"It has been well established t[...] [...] plurality of elders and that su[...] wanting elders and having q[...] This book bridges the gap by [...] suggestions for current leaders to develop faithful leaders to help shepherd the church of God. Those of you who aspire to serve as elders will benefit greatly from this book."

Benjamin L. Merkle, professor of New Testament and Greek,
Southeastern Baptist Theological Seminary

"I found this thoroughly biblical and eminently practical handbook a much-needed encouragement to be more intentional in this work, and I will profit from the clear model it presents."

Bill Kynes, senior pastor, Cornerstone Evangelical
Free Church, Annandale, VA

"The New Elder's Handbook offers a wealth of biblical wisdom and practical resources for disciple making and leadership development. I warmly recommend this helpful book to current and aspiring elders who desire to put into practice 2 Timothy 2:2 and entrust the gospel to faithful men who will be able to teach others also."

Brian J. Tabb, academic dean, Bethlehem College & Seminary;
elder, Bethlehem Baptist Church

"This is not just a how-to book on leadership. Rather, grounded in the Scriptures, it has a practical and pastoral focus, with learning taking place in community with others. I am elated this book is now available. Take up, read, apply, and see the leadership culture of the church be transformed."

Greg Strand, executive director of theology and credentialing,
Evangelical Free Church of America; adjunct professor of pastoral
theology, Trinity Evangelical Divinity School

"In The New Elder's Handbook Greg Scharf and Arthur Kok weave together robust theological engagement with eminently practical wisdom on the means of selecting and developing faithful Christian leaders. This work provided a timely reminder of the importance of character and competency in Christian leadership and is a welcome addition to the much-needed field of Christian leadership."

Malcolm Gill, lecturer in Greek, New Testament, and homiletics, Center
for Preaching and Pastoral Ministry, Sydney Missionary & Bible College

"Anyone who wants to raise up future leaders should read this book, first because of the program it offers and second because of the method it champions. Presenting theological and practical questions to a small group of future leaders and challenging them to come up with biblical answers will produce rapid growth in the lives of those you mentor."

Colin S. Smith, senior pastor, The Orchard Evangelical
Free Church, Arlington Heights, IL

"I recommend this book to men with a desire to become faithful elders and to the pastors who want to help shepherd them in the pursuit of that noble desire. This handbook is eminently usable, biblically rich, and very timely. I look forward to using it with my current elders and to training and discipling new elders with it for the future health of our church."

Glen Stevens, senior pastor, Salem Evangelical Free Church, Fargo, ND, and Moorhead, MN

"*The New Elder's Handbook* is an excellent resource for any church committed to the vital task of discerning and appointing qualified elders. Full of biblical wisdom and practical guidance, it not only casts a vision for this task but also offers a 'structured journey' (developed and used in a local-church context) that will help elders and prospective elders patiently discern God's will together for the health of our churches."

David H. F. Ng, program leader for Master of Missional Leadership, Melbourne School of Theology

"If you desire to see a thriving elder team in your local church, take advantage of the wisdom of this resource."

George Davis, senior pastor, Hershey Free Church, Hershey, PA

"Greg Scharf and Arthur Kok lay out a plan for selecting prospective elders and then rigorously discipling them in Christian practice and doctrine. You will not find a more thorough plan for the theological preparation of those entrusted with being shepherds of God's flock."

Lee Eclov, senior pastor, Village Church of Lincolnshire (IL); author of *Pastoral Graces*

"Those seeking to be equipped as elders as well as those already called as elders will benefit from the study guides and the rich reference material cited by the authors. Throughout this book, the authors' love of God, his Son Jesus Christ, his church, and his people shines brightly."

Pete Alle, elder and church vice-chair, The Orchard Evangelical Free Church, Arlington Heights, IL

"I teach pastors and church leaders in East Africa. Churches are multiplying, but the leadership of many is seriously deficient. If this book were read and applied, it would make a tremendous difference in that spiritually vital and strategic region of the world."

Jonathan Menn, director, Equipping Church Leaders–East Africa; author of *Biblical Eschatology*

"Many churches struggle to identify and train elders for the task of shepherding the church. Scharf and Kok offer a helpful resource that utilizes biblical examples and employs wisdom from pastoral experience to address this need. The health of the church is at stake, and this handbook is a valuable tool for the worthwhile task of raising up elders."

Nick Gatzke, senior pastor, Old North Church, Canfield, OH

THE NEW
ELDER'S
HANDBOOK

A BIBLICAL GUIDE TO DEVELOPING FAITHFUL LEADERS

GREG R. SCHARF
AND ARTHUR KOK

BakerBooks

a division of Baker Publishing Group
Grand Rapids, Michigan

© 2018 by Greg R. Scharf and Arthur Kok

Published by Baker Books
a division of Baker Publishing Group
PO Box 6287, Grand Rapids, MI 49516-6287
www.bakerbooks.com

Printed in the United States of America

Library of Congress Cataloging-in-Publication Data

Names: Scharf, Greg, author. | Kok, Arthur, 1980– author.
Title: The new elder's handbook : a biblical guide to developing faithful leaders / Greg R. Scharf and Arthur Kok.
Description: Grand Rapids : Baker Publishing Group, 2018.
Identifiers: LCCN 2017057408 | ISBN 9780801076343 (pbk.)
Subjects: LCSH: Elders (Church officers)
Classification: LCC BV680 .S33 2018 | DDC 253—dc23
LC record available at https://lccn.loc.gov/2017057408

In keeping with biblical principles of creation stewardship, Baker Publishing Group advocates the responsible use of our natural resources. As a member of the Green Press Initiative, our company uses recycled paper when possible. The text paper of this book is composed in part of post-consumer waste.

18 19 20 21 22 23 24   7 6 5 4 3 2 1

Contents

Introduction   7

Part 1 Vision

1. Who We Aspire to Be: What Characterizes Biblically Qualified Elders?   21
2. Understanding the Power: Ezra's Example   33
3. Making Progress: Moving Forward in Growth   39
4. Maximizing the Process: The Importance of Community   47
5. Identifying Potential Elders   57

Part 2 Training

6. Seventy-Five Questions for New or Prospective Elders   67

Part 3 Two Additional Discipleship Resources

7. Learning to Follow Jesus: A Thematic Resource for Discipling Others   145
8. BA (Biblical Agenda) in Christian Living: A Bible Study Resource for Discipling Others   165

Acknowledgments   179
Suggestions for Further Reading   181

Introduction

The saying is trustworthy: If anyone aspires to the office of overseer,
he desires a noble task.

1 Timothy 3:1

Every church needs qualified elders. They are a joy to a pastor,
sharing the load of leadership and the privileges of shepherding. They are a gift to a congregation, guarding the flock and
extending themselves in love. And they are God's plan for his church.
God loves the church so much that he gave his only Son to die for it.
He does not entrust such a treasure to a single individual; he deploys
a brotherhood, a cadre, a team so that the church is soaked in prayer,
led in wisdom, and fed by the Word. Healthy, faithful churches always
have a team of qualified, faithful leaders.

The essential nature of biblically qualified elders is clear in Scripture. Timothy and Titus were admonished by the apostle Paul to
appoint qualified elders, and Paul also spelled out the qualifications
(1 Tim. 3:1–7; Titus 1:5–9). The normal practice was to appoint elders in every town (Acts 14:23). This remains true today. Yet where
do such men come from?[1] Often they emerge organically. Pastors or
elders spot men who have credible faith, willingness to serve, and

1. Throughout we will refer to elders and elders in training as male. This reflects
our understanding of the criteria for elders in 1 Timothy 3 and Titus 1.

leadership gifts. But this does not always happen. What then? Or what if the number of qualified leaders is so small that serving elders feel they have signed up for a life sentence, with no one to take up this joyful yet sober responsibility after them? We know what happens: The expectations are lowered, and unqualified but available elders are appointed. Or perhaps the positions remain vacant, and God's people suffer.

Is there something better? How can qualified elders be *raised up*? How might someone *pursue the office* while guarding motivations, making progress, and trusting God to work? That's what this book is about.[2]

Raising Up Elders: A Pastor's Testimony

As an ordained pastor, I (Greg) have functioned as an elder for over forty years, beginning in that role before I was, well, an elder. After seminary I was an intern and then a curate—what we might call an assistant pastor—at a historic Anglican church: All Souls, Langham Place, in London, England. Then I was called to serve as an assistant minister in the venerable Knox Presbyterian Church in Toronto, Ontario, Canada. In both positions, I did more learning than teaching. Then, I was called to be the first full-time, permanent pastor of a newly planted church of some sixty people: Salem Evangelical Free Church in Fargo, North Dakota. My wife, Ruth, and I committed to this church to stay for ten years. We stayed for nineteen.

A few years into that time, I noticed that whenever I asked someone about his willingness to serve as an elder, he almost always said no. Some looked at the biblical qualifications and immediately ruled

---

2. We recognize that some of our readers will be pastors who aspire to equip and encourage elders. Other readers will be aspiring elders. Thus you may at times find some material most suited to the group of which you are not a part. In those cases, if you are a pastor, put yourself in the shoes of a prospective elder and envision them profiting from the material. If you are not a pastor or currently serving elder, that material will be more useful to you after you have worked through the training.

themselves out. Some were too busy. Others looked at the fine men who were already serving as elders and felt they could never measure up. Fargo is a university community, and we had many professors, business leaders, and seminary graduates in our church. So some prospective elders disqualified themselves because they perceived themselves to be not sufficiently educated.

As I prayed about the recurring problem of too few qualified elders, it occurred to me that the problem was not with them. It was with me. My thinking was too short-term. Even with the commitment to stick around for ten years, I still assumed that what this church would look like in thirty years was not my responsibility. I thought that was someone else's worry.

Once I repented of this selfish, shortsighted attitude, I did three things differently. First, I asked the Lord to lead me to men who might be willing to be *trained* as elders. I put them on a prayer list. Second, I did not ask them to *serve* as elders. Instead, I asked, "Assuming no promises—you're not promising to serve as an elder, and the congregation is not promising to appoint you—would you be willing to receive some training?" Third, I invited every prospective elder (with his wife) to a dessert night at our home, where I reviewed the expectations of a two-year elder training program. Then I sent them home to pray about this opportunity. I promised the wives that their husbands would be better husbands and fathers if they undertook and faithfully completed this training. Most of the men who came to such gatherings said yes.

I met weekly with the men in the elder training program. I took attendance and required each elder-in-training to spend at least half an hour a week answering the week's question and writing down what he discovered. I went through this two-year cycle three times, with a new group of trainees each time, although some repeated the course. When, during the final cycle, I was called to teach at Trinity Evangelical Divinity School, I left the church with at least thirty men who had received the training, and the church has reaped the rewards. One of those elders-in-training is now the senior pastor of the church.[3] Several of the others now serve in other ministries within and beyond that local church. I think of one university professor who faithfully submitted to the training and came to the conclusion, "I am a deacon, not an elder." He was right, and he has served faithfully in that role and others. Another adapted the material and used it in a church he pastored, and now he oversees denominational credentialing of pastors. Others serve in mission organizations, trades, businesses, and as teachers.

A Noble Aspiration

There are two main lessons that I hope you glean from my story. First, if you are a pastor, God can use you to raise up elders, especially if you are prayerfully deliberate, intentional, and strategic about it. This book, sharpened by my real-world pastoral experience, provides a resource that you can employ to do this. Second, and central to this book, if you aspire to be an elder, it is possible to *pursue the personal attributes* that would make you qualified for the office. Scripture says that anyone who aspires to the office desires a noble work (1 Tim. 3:1), and this book can help you fulfill that aspiration if God has given such a desire to you.

We hope this is you. We hope you have picked up this book because you aspire to be the sort of man who is biblically qualified to serve the church as an elder. Or, if you have been nominated or elected to be an elder, we hope you picked up this book because you passionately desire that the qualifications of eldership be *more consistently true of you*. This pleases our God. And we wrote this book to help you.

But even more, we wrote this book to encourage you. Perhaps you look at your pastor, or an elder you know, or a Christian writer whose books you love, and you think, "My life is miles away from that level of godliness. Sure, I wish I knew the Bible like that but—well, maybe

3. To be fair, he was already a seminary graduate in an intentional apprenticeship in the church during the year he joined the elders-in-training.

someday." If that's you, please hear us, dear brother: Those leaders did not reach that place accidentally. And it didn't happen magically. It happened through God's grace and the disciplined hard work of walking in the Spirit. Paul's testimony recorded in 1 Corinthians 15:10 captures the balance perfectly: "But by the grace of God I am what I am, and his grace toward me was not in vain. On the contrary, I worked harder than any of them, though it was not I, but the grace of God that is with me." It happened through slow, steady progress (1 Tim. 4:15). It happened for these pastors and elders because God set a desire in their hearts and they responded in the obedience of faith (Rom. 1:5; 16:26).

That can be you. Aspiring elder, seek first God's kingdom and his righteousness and ask him to add to you today everything you need to fulfill the noble aspiration to serve him as an elder in the church. Gather some brothers around you and start a journey working through this book. You will find that God works his growth in you. Let this book point you to Scripture in a way that helps you grow in knowledge of the Lord, in godly character, and in skills to serve God's people. Obey the prompting of God's Spirit, and let's get started.

A Resource for Your Journey

So how can this book help? First, it gives you a concrete, tailored training path to follow. If you want to be qualified to serve as an elder, if indeed God was speaking through someone who invited you to consider serving as an elder, don't quench the Spirit by doing nothing. This book will supply steps of obedience you can take to become qualified.

Second, this book will help you discern if you have the biblical qualifications. How you tackle the biblical study, relate to others who want to be elders, persevere, and relate to your wife and family during this time are some of the indicators of whether you have the durability, character, and gifting to serve the church faithfully as an elder.

Third, this book will help equip you to be the kind of person who *could* serve as an elder, whether or not the church appoints you to that noble task. In his fine book *Why Elders? A Biblical and Practical Guide for Church Members*,[4] Benjamin Merkle divides the qualifications for elders into three categories: situational, familial, and moral qualifications. In each domain, there is ample room for any man to grow. For instance, some of the traits he labels "situational qualifications"—desire to serve, ability to teach, not a recent convert, well thought of by outsiders—are matters that we can work on, and, more importantly, that God can work on for us and in us! The same is true to an even greater extent in the case of familial and moral qualifications.

Fourth, this book will drive you to your knees in humility and prayer. That is a good place for any man to be. Just the act of asking God to qualify you to be a teacher of and an example to the flock is a significant step in that direction.

Fifth, this book will foster intentional fellowship in the gospel. Sadly, in some churches, fellowship among men is mainly eating, talking about sports, or listening to inspiring speakers. Frankly, godly men want more; we want gospel fellowship where we feed on the Word of God, pray together, challenge each other, hold each other accountable, and serve together.

Sixth, this training will slow you down. First Timothy 5:22 says, "Do not be hasty in the laying on of hands, nor take part in the sins of others; keep yourself pure." What church leaders must *not* do—hastily appoint elders—you, as an aspiring elder, must not long for. There is no need to rush things. Eldership is not something anyone should jump into. You will benefit and the church will benefit by letting the Lord do his slow, steady work of sanctifying you.

4. Benjamin Merkle, *Why Elders? A Biblical and Practical Guide for Church Members* (Grand Rapids: Kregel Academic & Professional, 2009).

This Will Take Some Work

How will these benefits be achieved? The answer is simple but not easy. It will take some consecrated effort. You will need your Bible and a notebook. You will need to invest some focused time every week answering a question or doing an assignment posed by this book. You will need to be involved in some sort of ministry, such as leading a life group or teaching Sunday school; the best way to maximize the benefit of training is to put into practice what you are learning. You will need to commit to attendance and homework requirements and to those with whom you are training.

We achieved these benefits in ways that may not fit your situation, so don't take these as prescriptive; they are only descriptive. You will need to design your own approach that is tailored to your situation. Our groups met early every Tuesday morning. We met first in triplets for prayer and accountability, and we then came together for the training. The training time itself was as Socratic as I could make it. Each trainee was required to have attempted to answer the question of the week, and to write *something* (which I examined but did not grade). In the training hour, I invited individuals to share what they had written or some facet of what they had learned from the study. When necessary, I would chip in a thought or redirect the flow of discussion. I was always well prepared, but often the insights shared by the trainees were better than what I would have told them in a lecture. We ended on time. Just before people left for work, I pointed them to three or four helpful supplementary resources related to next week's question.

Doctrine + Life + the Ability to Teach

Questions are key to this training process. Instead of reading doctrinal information, resolving to shape up with regard to character, or contemplating some skills, we submit ourselves to Scripture and let the Word of God sanctify us as Jesus promised it would: "Sanctify them in the truth; your word is truth" (John 17:17).

So how did we decide which questions to include? Once again, the answer came from experience. Initially, I (Greg) simply worked through a list of fifty subjects that ordination candidates in our denomination study. I soon realized that this did not work very well because, on the one hand, there were no limits to some of these subjects, and, on the other hand, very few parishioners express their needs or concerns to an elder in terms of a systematic-theology category. So I tried to reword each doctrine as a question that a thoughtful member of the congregation might ask an elder. Even so, there wasn't much shape to the process. That is when I remembered Ezra 7:10, which I had memorized while being discipled by a Navigator: "For Ezra had set his heart to study the Law of the LORD, and to do it and to teach his statutes and rules in Israel." Doctrinal accuracy is indispensable for elders, but it is not enough to preserve the health of the church. Truth must shape life, and the truth must be taught to others.

Ezra 7:10 is not the only place in Scripture where these three sorts of qualifications are mentioned together. The apostle Paul wanted them to characterize every believer. He wrote to the Romans, "I myself am satisfied about you, my brothers, that you yourselves are full of *goodness*, filled with all *knowledge* and *able to instruct* one another" (Rom. 15:14, emphasis added). There you have them again: character, knowledge, and skill. Elders are meant to exemplify what all Christians should aim for. We are to be models to the flock as well as teachers of it. Consequently, some of the questions in this workbook address character issues and the disciplines that underlie them. Other questions relate to skills and practices entailed in teaching and discipling others. You will notice that fewer biblical texts relate to skills than doctrine and, accordingly, we will endeavor not to go beyond what is written (1 Cor. 4:6). Much mischief happens when we try to make the Bible address matters it is not intending to address! We include the skills category of questions to remind you that these skills are not irrelevant and need to be developed. There is wisdom in the body of Christ and beyond to help with that undertaking, just as an outsider of sorts—Moses's father-in-law, Jethro—offered wise counsel concerning how to handle complaints and conflicts (Exod. 18). Others in your trainee group or in the ministry that you are engaged in can help you foster these skills.

Here is what you can expect in each week's work: (1) a question (or series of questions) that you are to answer from Scripture, (2) some biblical passages that address this question, and (3) some additional resource materials that you could consult to help you place your answer within the pattern of sound doctrine (Titus 2:1). Each week's assignment may include many more texts than you have time to read, much less to study. Do what you can, but never focus on getting it all done at the expense of noticing the context of the passages. We decided to include enough passages to try to round out the biblical picture rather than making you look elsewhere if our list was too sparse. You will readily discover that many more texts might have been included. Feel free to add them as you go along. Although it is more cumbersome to look them up, we did not usually put the passages in canonical order. We tried to put them in some sort of logical order so that, if you read them in order and write down clear teachings and valid inferences, you will be moving in the direction of sound doctrine. The aim of including passages without telling you what to find in them is to provide you the opportunity to hone your ability to handle the Word of God. That won't happen if we spoon-feed you; it will only happen if we point you in a direction and let you do your own careful study. Your aim is to meet the standard of Titus 1:9: "He must hold firm to the trustworthy word as taught, so that he may be able to give instruction in sound doctrine and also to rebuke those who contradict it."

Just Begin

We understand that our readers do not all have the same starting point. Some are already careful readers of Scripture; others are not. Ideally, your pastor handles the Word well in the pulpit, letting it have its say in its way. If that is so, his sound interpretations and the hermeneutic that underlies them model how listeners should study the Bible on their own. If not, you will have some catching up to do. Whatever grade you would give yourself as a Bible reader and student, the only realistic growth strategy is to begin. Start where you are. Prayerfully use all the resources you can get your hands on, and share what you have learned with others in your group. Be teachable when they notice weaknesses, gaps, or imbalance in your answers. Ideally, every training group will have at least one mature, well-trained elder or pastor who can guide the process. Since elders are not to be new converts, our working assumption is that because they aspire to eldership or someone thinks they should be considered for eldership, members of these training groups are already reasonably well-taught. If you discover otherwise in this training process, that is a good thing. It is good for you as a trainee, because you can address and correct it; it is good for the church, because no church should have unqualified elders.

As you go forward, you will see that parts 1 and 2 of this book are primarily for aspiring elders. Part 1 is an on-ramp to the process, and part 2, the heart of the book, contains doctrinal, character-based, and skill-related questions. You will notice that we don't have separate categories for the questions on doctrine, character, and skills and disciplines. We keep them together because in real life these domains are always integrated. We don't do one, then the next, and finally the third; we do them all, all the time, as we will underscore in chapter 1. This book does not supply the answers except in the sense that it constantly points readers back to the Scriptures. The real value is not what it spells out for you but what it helps you to discover, understand, share, and obey.

Part 3 offers two discipleship resources that could be used in several ways. Chapter 7, "Learning to Follow Jesus," takes a thematic approach to the basics of the Christian life. Chapter 8, "BA (Biblical Agenda) in Christian Living," approaches similar basic topics by studying 2 Peter. As a pastor, you may want to use one of these resources in part 3 to disciple an individual to discover how motivated and consistent he is, as a preview to lengthier eldership training.[5] If you are an aspiring or current elder, these resources could be a tool to disciple others.

The development of this material has been a collaborative endeavor. It may be helpful for you to know that, in addition to this introduction, I (Greg) wrote chapters 1, 2, 5, 7, and 8. I also supplied the seventy-five questions in chapter 6 that constitute the heart of the book, though each of us took the lead on further developing some of them, and we both edited them and added Bible passages and resource materials. Arthur wrote chapters 3 and 4. We also offered editorial suggestions to each other throughout. We hope you hear our two individual voices and yet our shared passion that the church have biblically qualified elders.

Let me add a final introductory word. If you are an aspiring elder looking to use this resource to prepare yourself for service, remember to be thinking downstream spiritually: Don't merely think of all the benefits that *you* will receive, as if you were their final "consumer." Think of them all—the truths, the skills, the growing character—as things the Lord has entrusted to you for others to whom you minister. Some matters may feel overly elementary to you at this point in your growth, but they may not feel that way to someone you are seeking to equip or to those they are called to serve. Every elder is to guard the gospel so that we can do what Paul exhorted Timothy to do in 2 Timothy 2:2—namely, to entrust it to faithful men who will be able to teach others also. That is what this book aims to do, so that you can do the same. If you are a pastor, I hope you are already

5. If you are an aspiring elder, there are several ways that part 3 of this book may be useful to you as well. First, chapter 5 (on recruitment) may help as you seek to identify other men who can walk through this book with you. Once you have worked through the questions in part 2, you may want to use one of the discipleship resources in part 3 to disciple a younger believer. Alternatively, once your group has completed the questions in part 2, you may want to take on the challenge of discipling a few others together, using one of these resources as your guide. This would not only benefit your church but would also be a way to put into practice all that you learned in part 2.

passing on the gospel to others who will do the same. If not, this is a tailor-made opportunity to fulfill that calling. You may want to work through this material on your own first, adding biblical texts that come to mind or other contemporary references. Alternatively, you could go through it with those elders already serving, asking them to help you discern how it might best be employed in your setting. They could function as something of a pilot group. That would have the added advantage that they would not feel bypassed and would also benefit from the training.

PART 1

VISION

1

Who We Aspire to Be

What Characterizes Biblically Qualified Elders?

For Ezra had set his heart to study the Law of the LORD, and to do it and to teach his statutes and rules in Israel.

Ezra 7:10

I myself am satisfied about you, my brothers, that you yourselves are full of goodness, filled with all knowledge and able to instruct one another.

Romans 15:14

Knowledge, obedience, and teaching all belong together. I have already pointed out in the introduction that Ezra 7:10 and Romans 15:14 highlight these same three attributes. What Ezra exemplified, Paul observed and affirmed in the Christians at Rome, not merely in the leaders but in the followers too. Now I want to make the case that these three characteristics go together. I do this because the temptation that all prospective elders face is to play to our strengths and develop them to the exclusion of weaker areas.

At one level, building on our strengths is the very thing to do. Indeed, God designed the local church to have multiple elders so that each of us can do what God has gifted us to do. As we do that, we can trust God to raise up other elders who are strong where we are weak. That is a good strategy when it comes to spiritual gifts but not, I want to argue, when it comes to these three characteristics: knowledge, obedience, and teaching.

Knowledge and Obedience: A Virtuous Cycle

Let's start with the interplay between knowledge and obedience. In Scripture, these always belong together. To eliminate or shortchange either one undermines the other and may nullify it altogether. Here is why: Knowledge of Scripture is the way we come to know Christ and find salvation through him (2 Tim. 3:15). But the way we know Christ is rarely, if ever, *only* from reading or hearing the Bible. We also know Christ through the people who taught us the gospel. We are like Timothy, of whom Paul wrote, "But as for you, continue in what you have learned and have firmly believed, *knowing from whom you learned it* and how from childhood you have been acquainted with the sacred writings, which are able to make you wise for salvation through faith in Christ Jesus" (2 Tim. 3:14–15, emphasis added). To be the kind of elders who can teach the Bible, as 1 Timothy 3:2 and Titus 1:9 say we must be, we have to know it, and that requires study. But to teach it effectively, our lives must reflect it. Think of Philippians 4:9: "What you have learned and received and heard *and seen in me*—practice these things" (emphasis added).

Part of our teaching is what is seen in us through practice. Our lives are to show the transforming power of the gospel. That is why obedience (Ezra 7:10) and its fruit, goodness (Rom. 15:14)—what in this book we often call "character"—are necessary. Thankfully, this does not mean that we need to be perfect. Indeed, "we have this treasure in jars of clay, to show that the surpassing power belongs to God and not to us" (2 Cor. 4:7). But the jars-of-clay image means not that we may persist in sin but only that we are fragile, imperfect containers for the treasure of the gospel. That is why Paul could describe himself as the foremost of sinners (1 Tim. 1:15) and, without contradiction, could invite others to imitate him (1 Cor. 11:1).

Paul's strategy for the spread of the gospel was always verbal proclamation reinforced by visible, consistent demonstration of daily cross-bearing and the attendant resurrection power. Notice that Paul sent Timothy to Corinth not merely to restate the gospel message verbally but to provide the visual aid of a gospel-shaped life. Paul writes, "I urge you, then, be imitators of me. That is why I sent you Timothy, my beloved and faithful child in the Lord, to remind you of my ways in Christ, as I teach them everywhere in every church" (1 Cor. 4:16–17). Paul does not separate his message proclaimed "everywhere in every church" from his "ways in Christ." The two belong together. I don't think Timothy merely said, "Remember the sort of life Paul lived among you." I think that, along with verbal proclamation, he too lived that life and proclaimed the gospel message. He was Paul's faithful child in the faith and bore the family resemblance. People heard the gospel from him and saw the gospel displayed in his life.

We see this same dynamic in 1 Thessalonians 1–2. Paul considered the faith, hope, and love that he saw in the Thessalonian converts to be evidence that they had received the gospel as what it is, the word of God that goes to work in those who believe. But they did not just accept some doctrinally true ideas. The Thessalonian Christians became imitators of Paul, Silvanus, and Timothy (1:6) and also of the Judean churches they represented (2:14). Crucially, it was only because they were *imitators* that they could become *examples*: "And you became imitators of us and of the Lord, for you received the word in much affliction, with the joy of the Holy Spirit, so that you became an *example* to all the believers in Macedonia and in Achaia" (1 Thess. 1:6–7, emphasis added).

How to Increase in the Knowledge of God

Let's take this one step further. In Colossians 1, the apostle Paul rejoices that the Colossian Christians heard the true gospel and "understood the grace of God in truth" (1:6). That is doctrine. That prompted Paul to keep on praying "that you may be filled with the knowledge of [God's] will in all spiritual wisdom and understanding, so as to walk in a manner worthy of the Lord, fully pleasing to him: bearing fruit in every good work and increasing in the knowledge of God" (1:9–10). That is godliness.

What should strike us is not merely that we should be praying this for ourselves and others—we should—nor that we should be aiming for mere knowledge. Rather, we should be aiming for knowledge characterized by all wisdom and understanding. This is only part of the good news of this passage. When God grants this sort of knowledge in answer to prayer, we can walk in ways that please the Lord. These ways are not only that we bear fruit in every good work but also that we *increase in the knowledge of God*. The last phrase is significant because it affirms from another angle what I have been arguing in this chapter—namely, that we cannot really grow in our knowledge of God without good works. We should treat this as a positive promise. When we grow in this kind of wise, understanding knowledge and the good works that by definition accompany it, we will be able to further grow in wise knowledge. We might call this a virtuous cycle. Growth in wise knowledge leads to godliness, which leads to greater wise knowledge of God, which paves the way for growing godliness.

So don't think filling a notebook with truth is what you are aiming for as you engage in this training process. Yes, fill your notebook with truth, but when the truth in your notebook is the right kind of truth— that is, knowledge characterized by wisdom and understanding—that sort of gospel truth will bear the fruit of good works. That will put you in a position to see more truth in Scripture and to respond more fully to the God of truth, who will reward you with the capacity to keep growing into his likeness.

How Teaching Fits In

Now you might say at this point, "OK, I see the connection between truth and godliness. And I understand that you have to study to be able to be filled with knowledge. But where does the aptitude to teach come in?" Good question.

In Their Teaching, Elders Model What All Christians Are to Do

A case can be made that teaching is the duty of all Christians, and this is a major reason elders need to model it. One of the places we see this most clearly is Colossians 3:16: "Let the message of Christ dwell among you richly as you *teach and admonish one another* with all wisdom through psalms, hymns, and songs from the Spirit, singing to God with gratitude in your hearts" (NIV, emphasis added). Moreover, in the Sermon on the Mount, having affirmed absolutely that the law will not pass away until all is fulfilled, Jesus says, "Therefore whoever relaxes one of the least of these commandments and teaches others to do the same will be called least in the kingdom of heaven, but whoever *does* them and *teaches* them will be called great in the kingdom of heaven" (Matt. 5:19, emphasis added). I hope you noticed the connection between doing and teaching!

In addition, greatness in the kingdom always involves a missional stance that is not content just to know; it must also teach. Everyone is to know, do, and teach. The writer of Hebrews holds the same conviction that teaching is a normal part of the mature Christian life and that failure to obey the truth restricts the capacity to receive, obey, and teach. Listen to Hebrews 5:11–14, noting especially the phrase I have italicized.

About this we have much to say, and it is hard to explain, since you have become dull of hearing. For though *by this time you ought to be teachers*, you need someone to teach you again the basic principles of the oracles of God. You need milk, not solid food, for everyone who lives on milk is unskilled in the word of righteousness, since he is a child. But solid food is for the mature, for those who have their powers of discernment trained by constant practice to distinguish good from evil.

It does not follow that every Christian has the spiritual gift of teaching or is qualified to serve as an elder. The point rather is that when the gospel takes root and bears fruit, teaching in word and deed should follow, beginning in one's household. If it does not, something is amiss. Among those who have begun to teach by precept and example, some are gifted by God to teach the whole church and help protect it from false doctrine. These, if they meet the character and situational standards, should be considered for appointment as elders.

Teaching Is the Way Elders Guard the Gospel

There is another reason that teaching, along with and inseparable from knowledge and godly obedience, is an inherent qualification required of elders. When the apostle Paul charged Timothy to fulfill his ministry in Ephesus, an overarching responsibility he assigned was to guard the gospel. Without the gospel, there is no church and therefore no need for elders. Notice how Paul words his foundational instruction to Timothy: "Follow the pattern of the sound words that you have heard from me, in the faith and love that are in Christ Jesus. By the Holy Spirit who dwells within us, guard the good deposit entrusted to you" (2 Tim. 1:13–14).

Timothy's responsibility is to guard what has been entrusted to him. That entails "following" the pattern of sound words he heard from Paul. In other words, the received, apostolic, biblical truth is to be adhered to in all it taught and to be obeyed in all it required. As we learned earlier, this is not to be some wooden, by-the-numbers mastery of ideas or concepts but is to be "in the faith and love that are in Christ." We can obey this injunction only by virtue of God's grace manifested in our union with Christ, which brings with it the gift of the Holy Spirit, who indwells us and enables us to guard the gospel. That was the apostle Paul's testimony: "But by the grace of God I am what I am, and his grace toward me was not in vain. On the contrary, I worked harder than any of them, though it was not I, but the grace of God that is with me" (1 Cor. 15:10).

How do we do that? How do we guard the gospel? Scripture offers several strategies, but the one that I see as key here, the one that reinforces the necessity of teaching, is in 2 Timothy 2:2–7:

> And what you have heard from me in the presence of many witnesses entrust to faithful men, who will be able to teach others also. Share in suffering as a good soldier of Christ Jesus. No soldier gets entangled in civilian pursuits, since his aim is to please the one who enlisted him. An athlete is not crowned unless he competes according to the rules. It is the hard-working farmer who ought to have the first share of the crops. Think over what I say, for the Lord will give you understanding in everything.

Yes, there are important verses in between (1:15–2:1), but the repetition of "what you have heard from me" in 1:13 and 2:2 ties the *command* to guard the gospel in 1:13–14 with the *means* to do so in 2:2–7. How do we guard the gospel? We guard it ultimately not by hoarding it but by entrusting it. *The best way to keep the gospel safe is to faithfully teach it to those who are equally able to teach it to others.*

This will not happen without the faithful living that these verses describe. We are to live like the undistracted soldier who wants to please his commander, like the disciplined athlete who doesn't break the rules, and like the hard-working farmer who shares the harvest. Each of these people is purposeful. The soldier fights to please his commander; the athlete runs to win; the farmer toils to share the crop. We too live this sort of disciplined life for a purpose.

We do it to entrust the gospel we heard to as many faithful people as possible.

Some years ago I experienced a vivid example of the importance of this principle. I was preaching in Romania in the days before the fall of the dictator Nicolae Ceaușescu. The church was under serious persecution. A faithful pastor had escaped into temporary exile to try to serve the Romanian church from abroad and then return when he could. He needed his few Romanian theological books but had not been able to take them with him in his escape from the country. I was asked if I could put them in my suitcase and take them to him in London. I was willing, but it was too risky in those days. If I had been challenged in customs as I left the country—as I had been once before—the books would have been lost and fellow Christians might have been in greater danger.

In the providence of God, that same week a choir from London was singing in the same church where I was preaching. Each member of the choir agreed to tuck one book or paper into his or her luggage and to reassemble the library when they got to London. The plan worked; the library got to the pastor. Even if one or two or five choristers had had their bags searched and the materials confiscated, most of the library would have made it through. We need not worry that the gospel will not survive or the church will not be built, given Christ's promise of Matthew 16:18, but we do have a key role to play in God's work. We guard the gospel by teaching faithful people who are able to teach others also. We want the gospel to get through to the next generation and to the ends of the earth. Teaching is integral to guarding the gospel.

Doctrine and Life Work Together in Biblically Qualified Elders

Having affirmed that doctrine, character, and skills must go together in the lives of elders, look now at the texts that speak directly of the qualifications of elders. First Timothy 3:1–7 mainly describes observable character traits required of overseers—the same office as elder.[1] Elders must be above reproach. Indeed, people both inside and outside the church should be able to affirm that elders are above reproach. But in verse 2, nestled among these character traits, is the *aptitude to teach*. It is listed not as an optional extra but as a necessity. "Therefore an overseer *must* be . . . able to teach" (emphasis added). The fact that the aptitude to teach and unimpeachable character are bundled together, and that the emphasis is on public and private goodness, is important. Character alone is not enough; the capacity to teach by itself is insufficient. Truth must be exemplified; the power of the gospel must be seen as well as heard. That is why Paul exhorts Timothy to watch his life *and* doctrine (1 Tim. 4:16). Elders have to watch both, and we cannot watch our teaching unless we "practice these things [and immerse ourselves] in them" (1 Tim. 4:15). That is also why Paul had to describe his sufferings to the Colossian Christians (Col. 1:24–2:5). Without visible evidence of his transformed life, his listeners would not have the whole message.

Titus 1:5–9 directs Titus, who like Timothy is an apostolic representative, to appoint elders who are above reproach (1:6–7). Here, however, the teaching role is expanded: "He must hold firm to the trustworthy word as taught, so that he may be able to give instruction in sound doctrine and also to rebuke those who contradict it" (1:9). That verse alone specifies four responsibilities of each qualified elder. First, the verse addresses what he must believe: he must believe sound doctrine as received from the apostles, and not some dubious alternative. Second, the verse addresses how he must believe it: he must hold firmly to this apostolic doctrine, not with some shaky grasp but with a firm one, really believing it. Third, he must grasp it well enough that he can teach it. Fourth, he must be able to rebuke those who contradict it; that is, he must not only know the boundaries of

1. Note that in Acts 20:17 and 28 the terms "elders" and "overseers" refer to the same people. These leaders are to "shepherd" the flock. The words used there are from the same word group as "pastor." Similarly, 1 Timothy 3:1–7 speaks of "overseers"; Titus 1:5–9 speaks of "elders."

sound doctrine well enough to recognize heresy but he must also have the courage to name such false teaching and repudiate it.

As always, context is key to application. Notice particularly that Titus, having spoken of refuting false teaching, now in 1:10–16 describes specific false teachers, not mainly in terms of their doctrinal errors, which seem to be Jewish myths of some sort, but in terms of their character. They are insubordinate, empty talkers, motivated by shameful gain, with both minds and consciences defiled. They are unfit for any good work. We should not be surprised that a defiled mind and a defiled conscience go together. This is because an ungodly life (leading to a guilty conscience) and misleading doctrine (readily accepted by a defiled mind) feed each other. By contrast, in Titus 2 Paul exhorts Titus to teach what accords with sound doctrine and then proceeds to describe attitudes and behaviors that adorn the gospel (2:1–10). Lest Titus miss the connection, Paul exhorts him, "Show yourself in all respects to be a model of good works, and in your teaching show integrity, dignity, and sound speech that cannot be condemned, so that an opponent may be put to shame, having nothing evil to say about us" (2:7–8).

Paul is not alone in insisting on the connection between life and doctrine, between knowledge and character. In 1 Peter 5:1–4, Peter exhorts elders to shepherd the flock of God as God wills. Peter tells us how to do this by underscoring three things to avoid, each of which is to be replaced by a godly approach to exercising oversight. First, we are to shepherd God's flock not under compulsion but willingly. Second, we are to do so not for shameful gain but with sincere eagerness. Third, we are not to domineer over people but rather to be an example to them. The promise that follows is that when we do so we can anticipate receiving the "unfading crown of glory" (5:4).

What I hope you notice is that these largely attitudinal or motivational prohibitions and exhortations concerning how elders are to discharge their duties are embedded in doctrine. Among the doctrinal truths affirmed in the immediate context of this passage are the necessity of gospel obedience (1 Pet. 4:17); the faithfulness of the Creator

(4:19); the historicity of the incarnation (5:1); the reality of glory to come (5:1, 4); the enmity and reality of Satan (5:8); the abundance of God's grace (5:10); and much more. Only those who stand firm in the *true* grace of God (5:12) can live the life he calls us to live. We have to know it before we can live it, and we have to live it in order to adequately teach it. If you have any lingering doubt that truth and godliness are inseparable, read 2 Peter. Peter repeatedly exposes and rebukes *un*godliness that is always the bedfellow of *false* teaching.

Now that you have seen this pattern, I hope that wherever you turn in the Bible, you will see the connection between truth and godliness. It is, I dare say, on almost every page. Look for it and let it strengthen your resolve to grow in grace—in both the truth of God's grace and the life that you can live because of it. This organic connection should not be something that intimidates us, making us feel that God is asking too much of us. Instead, we should recall that our good God designed the universe so that we can experience the abundant life for which he made us.

Aim for All Three

So as you let the Bible help you integrate study, obedience, and teaching, thank God for the way that he has designed both you and the task of equipping you to serve the church. Yes, one week focus on doctrinal truth to be guarded and taught, and the next week zero in on a skill to be learned, and the third week give yourself to growth in some facet of your character, but rejoice that they all work together by design. Make Philippians 1:9–11 your prayer for yourself and those with whom you partner in this undertaking.

> And it is my prayer that your love may abound more and more, with knowledge and all discernment, so that you may approve what is excellent, and so be pure and blameless for the day of Christ, filled with the fruit of righteousness that comes through Jesus Christ, to the glory and praise of God.

2

Understanding the Power

Ezra's Example

For the good hand of his God was on him. For Ezra had set his heart.

Ezra 7:9c–10a

We have seen how knowledge, character, and teaching go together. Now we consider how this worked in Ezra's life. We have already looked at what Ezra set his heart to do—namely, "to study the Law of the LORD, and to do it and to teach his statutes and rules in Israel." Now we need to explore the words "set his heart" and how that resolve relates to God's good hand on Ezra. This is important, because you are about to launch into a demanding process of training. It won't be sustainable if you simply drift into it or are doing it under some misguided compulsion. With the Lord's help you can do it, but it won't happen by accident. Like Ezra, you must set your heart on this undertaking. Having said that, it would be seriously misleading if you had the impression that your resolve is the most important element in what is about to happen. It isn't. What God is going to do in and through you will make the difference. But there is a connection between the two that we need to explore.

God's Good Hand Is Active

God's Sovereignty in Ezra's Life

The story of Ezra gives us a clear view of the sovereignty of God. God's people returned from Babylonian captivity in three waves. The first group of returnees, under the leadership of Zerubbabel, focused on trying to rebuild the temple. The second, led by Ezra some sixty years later, mainly sought to reestablish Mosaic law as the center of life for the covenant people. Nehemiah came later to rebuild the walls of Jerusalem. A good study Bible will remind you of the dates and details of Ezra's day and his role. Most of Ezra's story is in Ezra 7–10, but, significantly, Nehemiah 8 records an occasion when Ezra preached the Word and the people heard it.[1]

We see right from the outset of the story of Ezra that God is already at work keeping his promise to his people well before Ezra is introduced into the narrative: "In the first year of Cyrus king of Persia, that the word of the LORD by the mouth of Jeremiah might be fulfilled, the LORD stirred up the spirit of Cyrus king of Persia" (Ezra 1:1). Cyrus's decree, which he put in writing, was that he, Cyrus, a pagan king, would facilitate and finance the rebuilding of the temple of the Lord in Jerusalem (Ezra 1:2–4). God was also at work in family leaders to stir them up to join the project and to add their financial support (1:5–6; 2:68). God united the people (3:1) and enabled Jeshua and Zerubbabel and their kin to rebuild the altar, offer sacrifices, and keep the feasts as the Mosaic law prescribed (3:2–7). They went on, with the help of the priests and Levites, to lay the foundation of the temple of the Lord (3:8–13). Ezra 4–6 records opposition and a stoppage of the work on the temple but also that God

---

1. In the Hebrew Bible, the books of Ezra and Nehemiah are one volume.

worked through Darius the king and Tattenai the governor to enable the returned exiles to finish the temple and celebrate the Passover. Ezra 6:22 ends this part of the account: "And they kept the Feast of Unleavened Bread seven days with joy, for the LORD had made them joyful and had turned the heart of the king of Assyria to them, so that he aided them in the work of the house of God, the God of Israel." God was already at work. God used pagan rulers, but he superintended the whole process, including the timing: "But the eye of their God was on the elders of the Jews, and [their enemies] did not stop them [from building] until the report should reach Darius and then an answer be returned by letter concerning it" (5:5). It is always wise to remember that God was at work long before he woke us up to our responsibilities. In his sovereignty, he arranges things to accomplish his good purposes and keep his promises.

Ezra 7:1 tells us that time has passed—scholars reckon it was about sixty years—and introduces Ezra to us. His pedigree establishes that he is a descendant of Aaron and therefore in the priestly line (7:2–5). But Ezra was not qualified just by birth; he was also qualified by study: "He was a scribe skilled in the Law of Moses that the LORD, the God of Israel, had given" (7:6a). The word the ESV renders "skilled" could just as fairly be translated "ready." He knew his Bible; he didn't need a pocket concordance (or a Bible app). He was a man of the Book. That was important, but the most essential truth is highlighted in what follows: "and the king granted him all he asked, *for the hand of the LORD his God was on him*" (emphasis added). Ezra's favor before King Artaxerxes is set forth as a *result* of God's good hand being on Ezra. Here Ezra's skill in the Word is not explicitly linked to God's hand. When we come to Ezra 7:9–10, there does appear to be a connection: "For on the first day of the first month he began to go up from Babylonia, and on the first day of the fifth month he came to Jerusalem, for the good hand of his God was on him. For Ezra had set his heart to study the Law of the LORD, and to do it and to teach his statutes and rules in Israel." The Lord's good hand is tied to the safe four-month trip to Jerusalem in verse 9, but at the beginning of verse 10 the "for"—literally, "because"—leaves the impression that this success under God's good hand is somehow the fruit of Ezra's having set his heart to study, do, and teach God's Word.

God Is Already at Work in You

How do we connect God's sovereignty and the obedience of his people? Some things are fixed points in God's plan. God will accomplish his purposes for his world. Christ will build his church, and the gates of hell will not prevail against it (Matt. 16:18). The kingdoms of the world will become the kingdom of God and of his Christ (Rev. 11:15). In answer to prayer, he will raise up servants to work in his fields (Matt. 9:37–38). The ascended Christ gives gifted people to the church to equip them to build up the church (Eph. 4:9–16). In all his people he works by his Spirit "both to will and to work for his good pleasure" (Phil. 2:13b).

Could God have accomplished his purposes for his people without Ezra? Of course. But he worked in Ezra's heart to move him to seek his Word, to do it, and to teach its ideas and its requirements. That is still the way God works. Your heart set on knowing, obeying, and teaching God's Word is not so much a prerequisite of receiving training toward eldership as it is an indication that God is already at work in you both to will and to work toward this good end. If that heart resolve is not there, ask God to grant it to you by his Holy Spirit. Because he loves his church, this is a gift that he is delighted to give. Getting this truth deeply embedded into our minds is important because it will help determine to whom we give glory or credit for anything good that happens in this process. The book of Ezra makes it clear that the success and the glory belonged to God.

What to Expect from God's Good Hand

We cannot leave Ezra without an encouraging look at the kinds of things we can expect when God's good hand is on someone. Here is a mere sample of the things God did in and through Ezra. Take them as reminders of what he delights to do in and through us by his own presence with us.

God granted Ezra a successful journey from Babylon to Jerusalem: "For on the first day of the first month he began to go up from Babylonia, and on the first day of the fifth month he came to Jerusalem, for the good hand of his God was on him" (Ezra 7:9). We should not forget that God takes care of mundane things when we seek first his kingdom and righteousness, as Matthew 6:33 tells us.

God moved King Artaxerxes to authorize Ezra's teaching—and supply magistrates to enforce it. Artaxerxes recognized its source and its wisdom: "And you, Ezra, according to the wisdom of your God that is in your hand, appoint magistrates and judges who may judge all the people in the province Beyond the River, all such as know the laws of your God. And those who do not know them, you shall teach" (Ezra 7:25). God can and does use those in authority, as he used a mere town clerk in Ephesus (Acts 19:35), and we should ask him to do so in our context as well (1 Tim. 2:1–2).

God showed his love and gave Ezra courage and favor in recruiting fellow leaders: "Blessed be the Lord, the God of our fathers, who put such a thing as this into the heart of the king, to beautify the house of the Lord that is in Jerusalem, and who extended to me his steadfast love before the king and his counselors, and before all the king's mighty officers. I took courage, for the hand of the Lord my God was on me, and I gathered leading men from Israel to go up with me" (Ezra 7:27–28). Ask God to grant you favor with "leading men" in the congregation whom you can invite to consider serving the church. He can prompt them to follow you as you follow Christ (1 Cor. 11:1).

God supplied qualified servants for the house of the Lord: "And by the good hand of our God on us, they brought us a man of discretion, of the sons of Mahli the son of Levi, son of Israel, namely Sherebiah with his sons and kinsmen" (Ezra 8:18). Not every role is a highly visible one. Ask the Lord to supply those faithful behind-the-scenes workers who will expedite ministry. I have seen him answer this prayer countless times in truly remarkable ways.

God gave Ezra integrity and the capacity to trust him for protection: "For I was ashamed to ask the king for a band of soldiers and horsemen to protect us against the enemy on our way, since we had told the king, 'The hand of our God is for good on all who seek him, and the power of his wrath is against all who forsake him'" (Ezra 8:22). This does not mean we never make use of governmental protection. Ezra and Nehemiah did so, as did the apostle Paul (Acts 16:37). It does teach us that when we have publicly committed to trust God and he is in it, he will act to get glory for his name when our practice is consistent with our profession.

God granted deliverance from enemies: "Then we departed from the river Ahava on the twelfth day of the first month, to go to Jerusalem. The hand of our God was on us, and he delivered us from the hand of the enemy and from ambushes by the way" (Ezra 8:31). God does not deliver all of his people *from* death; some he delivers *through* death. Whichever way he chooses, he will deliver us from our enemies when they are his enemies too (Rom. 8:38–39).

You get the picture. God went before Ezra and went with him. He was at work *in* Ezra as well as at work *for* Ezra. With God at work in all these ways, we may be tempted to sit back and watch him, to let him get on with it. God could do it that way. He moved Cyrus, Artaxerxes, and Darius to do what he wanted. He can speak through rocks and donkeys if necessary. It seems, however, that his preferred strategy is to start generations earlier and fashion someone who will by the Spirit's enabling respond to his gracious initiative and do his will. Then he works through them. You can be one of those people. Take some time today to pray that Ezra 7:10 would deeply characterize you.

3

Making Progress

Moving Forward in Growth

From whom the whole body, nourished and held together by its ligaments and tendons, grows with growth from God.

Colossians 2:19b CSB

So far we have made the case that Ezra's three noted characteristics—knowledge, obedience, and ability to teach—belong together. They interweave and support one another, characterizing a leader that God uses to shepherd his people. We have also seen that God tends to plant the desire to *be characterized* by these elements in the hearts of men he would call to serve as elders. In this chapter we make the case that it is not just the desire to *be characterized* by these three elements that marks a qualified elder; it is the commitment to *pursue* them. This pursuit isn't easy; it is not quick; there are no shortcuts. But oh how often we wish there were!

When I (Arthur) was a child, my family would occasionally take long trips at Christmas to visit my relatives on the East Coast. My parents would bundle the kids into coats, fasten the seat belts, and start driving, usually around nine o'clock at night. My eyes would droop, I would nod off to sleep, and the next thing I knew it was morning and we were pulling into my aunt and uncle's driveway. Those trips were magic! I would close my eyes, and we were there! Now as a dad and a driver, I am painfully aware that you do not reach the destination without the journey. That means we cannot zip to *being* a person who is a biblically qualified elder without embracing the journey of *becoming* one.

Clearly you have taken this to heart if you are reading this book. You are not one who is stagnant, just hoping that you will grow in biblical maturity. You have set your heart on this endeavor and are pursuing it by reading and working through this book. And by God's grace, you will make progress because his hand is on you and you are taking action.

What you will find here is a structured journey, through which you can move from where you are to a place where you reflect more of the qualities of an elder. Central to the journey is a series of questions that qualified elders need to be able to answer. If you can explain the doctrine and godly habits that characterize genuine faith to the others in your group, then, at the very least, you will be able to teach—since that is basically what you will be doing. We also trust that this level of understanding will be accompanied by a growing evidence of godly character.

Seven Foundational Principles of Christian Spiritual Growth

So how can we grow in the direction of being qualified as an elder? Before we summarize our process in more detail, we need to briefly outline seven foundational principles of Christian spiritual growth. As we go along, you will see that these principles shape and inform everything we suggest in the rest of the book.

Only True Christians Experience Spiritual Growth

Only those who are truly converted—who are made alive by the Holy Spirit and in Jesus—can move forward in godliness (Titus 3:4–7; Eph. 2:5; 5:8; John 15:1–8). The Bible describes those who are not united to Jesus Christ by faith as blind (2 Cor. 4:4), enslaved to sin (John 8:34), hostile to God (Rom. 8:7), and dead (Eph. 2:1). Such people cannot grow spiritually. Thus, any who would pursue spiritual growth should begin by humbly seeking to discern the presence of authentic new birth (John 3:3–8).

God Gives Spiritual Growth

If we grow, it is thanks to God, not us. Believers ultimately grow "with growth from God" (Col. 2:19 CSB). Even human leaders cannot take credit for spiritual growth. In speaking of the church in Corinth, Paul writes, "I planted, Apollos watered, but God gave the growth. So then neither he who plants nor he who waters is anything, but only God who gives the growth" (1 Cor. 3:6–7). We are called to pursue growth actively, but with the foundational recognition that it is God who enables and works in us (Phil. 2:12–13).

God Grows Christians as They Spend Time in His Word

Paul writes that "all Scripture is inspired by God and is profitable for teaching, for rebuking, for correcting, for training in righteousness, so that the man of God may be complete, equipped for every good work" (2 Tim. 3:16–17 CSB). Time spent in Scripture shapes and forms us so that we might be righteous and godly servants of Christ. The Lord Jesus's high-priestly prayer reflects this reality: "Sanctify them in the truth; your word is truth" (John 17:17).

God Grows Christians as They Spend Time in Prayer

Christians are commanded to pray (Col. 4:2; 1 Thess. 5:17). This is because prayer is a means of intimacy with and dependence on

God. Jesus often took time away from the disciples to pray (Matt. 14:23; Mark 1:35; Luke 6:12). He stressed the personal nature of God when he taught the disciples to pray (Matt. 6:9), and he modeled this in his own prayers (Luke 22:41; John 11:41; 17:1). Those who pray cultivate intimacy with God, deepening the relationship and nourishing the bond through which all growth occurs. More than this, prayer teaches us to lean into what is ultimately true: that God is God, and we are not. He is king, sovereign, full of resources, and worthy of praise; we are servants, dependent, needy, and called to praise him (1 Chron. 16:11; James 5:13; Ps. 103:1–5). The more the posture of our prayer life shapes our daily life, the more spiritually mature we are.

This Growth Happens under the Guidance and Teaching of the Holy Spirit

It is the Spirit who uses the Word and prayer to sanctify believers (1 Pet. 1:2). He transforms our character, making believers an acceptable offering to God (Rom. 15:14–16); he interprets our prayers (Rom. 8:26); and he teaches us the wisdom of God (1 Cor. 2:6–12). It is because of the Holy Spirit that Christians can behold Christ, which is what transforms us into the image of Jesus (2 Cor. 3:18–4:16). Disciplined reading of God's Word and prayer are good, but without the work of the Spirit of Christ, even those disciplines will not have the intended effect. When our minds are set on the Spirit and we live according to the Spirit, we can live lives that please God (Rom. 8:8–9).

This Growth Happens in the Community of God's People

Christians are not isolated individuals; we are part of an organic body, of which Christ is the head. Other believers sharpen us (Prov. 27:17), teach us (Rom. 15:14), carry our burdens (Gal. 6:2), admonish us (Col. 3:16), encourage us (1 Thess. 4:18; Heb. 3:13), spur us to love and good works (Heb. 10:24–25), and pray for us (James 5:16).

We cannot expect to grow significantly if we are not in intimate relationship with other believers.

This Growth Happens over Time

When the Father rescues us from the domain of darkness and transfers us into the kingdom of the Son he loves (Col. 1:13), he does not immediately fully transform us into the image of Christ, although that is the goal (Rom. 8:29; 2 Cor. 3:18). We grow up into Christ over time (Eph. 4:15), and the process isn't complete until we see Jesus face-to-face (1 John 3:2). This is why the Bible constantly challenges us to persevere (Heb. 6:11) and continue to run the race of faith (1 Cor. 9:24–27).

With these foundational principles in mind, we now turn to the structured journey that we suggest in this book. We will outline the process by describing the four core elements and by detailing three more that are strongly suggested.

Four Core Elements

The four core elements to the elder training process are questions, personal work in the Word, prayer, and time.

Questions

As Greg shared in the introduction, he has developed a list of questions that are particularly relevant to elders. They are questions for which elders need to have clear, succinct, biblically grounded answers. They cover issues of church practice, Christian doctrine, godly living, and biblical worldview. These questions form the heart of this book and of the elder training process. They are meant to drive you into God's Word and to lead you to a deeper knowledge of God's truth that transforms your life and equips you to impart that truth to others.

Personal Work in the Word

We have provided a list of Scripture references for each question. We encourage you to read these Scriptures in their respective contexts, meditate on them, digest them, and let them inform, shape, and define your answers to each question. Why? Because your answers must first and foremost be biblical. They must also be firmly held, to paraphrase the requirement of Titus 1:9. (Some of your answers will be tentative, because at this stage you humbly admit that your grasp of biblical truth is partial. Other answers will be held more lightly because the biblical text itself does not speak definitively to the question we pose.) And they must be your answers in your own words. Submissive time in the Bible will give you faithful, credible, and personal answers to questions you might face in leadership. Congregation members will appreciate your answers when you humbly invite them to test all things and hold on to what is good (1 Thess. 5:21).

If we want to grow in knowledge, character, and godliness—everything that should characterize an elder—there is no substitute for being shaped inwardly and outwardly by Scripture.

Prayer

Prayer is essential to effectively digest the Scriptures and produce faithful answers to questions. The entire training process will fall far short of producing the kind of knowledge and character demonstrated by Ezra if you do not constantly look to the Lord in prayer (1 Tim. 2:8). Prayer acknowledges our deep dependence on God (Phil. 4:6), our need for the Holy Spirit (Rom. 8:26), our desire to grow (Luke 17:5; 1 Pet. 2:2), and our deep confidence in God (Matt. 7:11; Rom. 12:12; Ps. 17:6). It is a demonstration of our faith and must soak every step in this training process.

Time

Lastly, you must take time to answer the questions. We recommend that you answer one question per week, spending time daily in the Word and in prayer over the listed Scriptures. At this rate, the process will take at least one year and probably longer. Why? First, time allows God to cement the knowledge in you. We all know the experience of cramming for a test and then forgetting most of the material within a week. That's not what we want here! We want to wrestle with the material and remember the conclusions we have reached. Don't forget: one goal of this training process is that at the end of your journey, you will be able to answer actual questions from congregation members. Second, time allows the Holy Spirit to work. Again, we're not aiming for big heads; we are aiming for transformed character and to be thoroughly equipped equippers (2 Tim. 2:2; 3:16–17).[1]

Three Strongly Suggested Elements

If you aspire to be an elder someday and want to pursue training to that end, you will need the four core elements outlined above. If you pursue these by yourself, you will get some benefit from the undertaking. That is better than nothing. But the benefits will be far greater if you add three strongly suggested elements. These are an active ministry of the Word, peer relationships, and a mentor.

An Active Ministry of the Word

As you are able, seek out a setting in which you can teach and handle God's Word within your church. This could be a small-group Bible study, Sunday school class, or discipleship group. This arena will allow you to practice teaching and solidify what you are learning

---

1. Paul Tripp has an excellent chapter on this topic: "Big Theological Brains and Heart Disease," in *Dangerous Calling: Confronting the Unique Challenges of Pastoral Ministry* (Wheaton: Crossway, 2012).

through this process. Elders are shepherds of God's people. Why not pursue an opportunity for teaching God's Word and caring for God's flock *right now*?

Peer Relationships

God does not intend that his people pursue spiritual growth in isolation. We need others in the body of Christ! If you are an aspiring elder, we strongly encourage you to find at least two or three other men to walk on this journey with you. Commit to one another. Set a weekly time when you will come together to discuss your answers, sharpen your knowledge, and pray for one another. Hold one another accountable to make progress toward the example of Ezra. You will find yourself built up by one another and stirred to pursue Christlikeness together.

A Mentor

In addition to godly peers, a mature mentor who knows the Bible and models godliness is invaluable. Consider asking your pastor to meet with you and your peers weekly. You will each produce your answers separately and then come together under his spiritual guidance. When Greg did this in North Dakota, he met with men early one morning per week to review answers. People gathered in groups of three to pray for one another for thirty minutes, either before or after the meeting, depending on their work schedules.

Do you feel you have a long way to go to measure up to the example of Ezra, not to mention the example of Christ? Are you far from the character and knowledge required for elders according to 1 Timothy 3 and Titus 1? Take heart! God promises to work his growth in us as we submit to the means he prescribes. In this chapter we've looked at a specific process that we recommend you use to pursue the growth that God desires. In the next chapter we look at the way that community and relationships allow you to maximize this process as you work through the rest of the book.

4

Maximizing the Process

The Importance of Community

Carry one another's burdens; in this way you will fulfill the law of Christ.

Galatians 6:2 CSB

Any man who desires to be characterized by knowledge, obedience, and the ability to teach and who is committed to pursue such characteristics is indeed on the pathway to godly leadership. However, progress along this pathway will be greatly affected by the subject of this chapter: Christian community. If you are walking on this path alone, your progress will be slow, or even null; if you are walking with peers beside you, mentors before you, and intercessors lifting you up, God will grow you in ways only he can anticipate.

Challenges Ahead

Here is the sobering truth: this pathway is not smooth. If you are committed to it, if you want to grow in knowledge and obedience and skill, you'll face some serious challenges.

You will find yourself under spiritual attack. Our enemy despises those who pursue the likeness of our Lord, and he wants you to quit. You will find temptations thrust in your path, opportunities to stray, and accusations in your heart that strike close to home. You are aiming to be a captain in Christ's army, so Satan will be aiming at you. But we need not be outwitted by him (2 Cor. 2:11).

You will become more aware of your sin than ever before. How could it be otherwise? The Holy Spirit wants to refine you, sharpen you. He will reveal ignorance, ingrained selfishness, shallow doctrine, unhelpful indulgences, unrealized prejudice, secret idols—all so that by his grace and power, these might be mortified and you might be purified (2 Tim. 2:21). How precious! Yet the sin that you will find in the recesses of your own heart will cause godly sorrow and deep conviction (2 Cor. 7:10).

And you will find that at times your own heart is against you. If you are united to Christ, you are a new creation (2 Cor. 5:17). Sin no longer *reigns* in you (Rom. 6:12–14), but it does *remain* (Gal. 5:16–18). The desire you feel to pursue a life like Ezra's, the conviction stirring in your soul right now, will wax and wane. At times, you will be your own worst enemy.

For all these reasons, we urge you not to pursue this life alone. In chapter 3 we noted that spiritual growth happens in the community of God's people. This is God's design. If we are isolated, we just won't grow as we might. Consider this: A plant may grow on the edge of a cliff, buffeted by the wind, its roots gnarled around rocks as it clings to them for dear life. But compare that to a plant in a greenhouse, where temperature is controlled, nutrients are added, soil is ideal, protection is given, and care is provided. Which will flourish? The community of God's people is the greenhouse God gives us for maximum spiritual growth.

Why Community Helps

Let's lean in to your potential situation: You have been sincerely converted. You have the Spirit of God in you. As you have read this book so far, you feel a desire to actively pursue the qualifications for being an elder. Surely you should do this. Yet our advice is that if you do not have at least two or three others who will commit to do this with you, you should not. You should wait until you can process and pursue this with others. Why are other believers so central to spiritual growth, particularly as it relates to pursuing and discerning the qualifications to be an elder?

Here are ten reasons for you to consider.

1. Caution—Other Believers Can Tell You "No" or "Wait"

Perhaps you should not undertake this process right now, for a reason you cannot see clearly. Perhaps you have a compulsive sin that you need to battle and mortify (Rom. 8:13). Perhaps your marriage or home life requires special attention, and you should focus on serving your family for the next few years (1 Tim. 3:4–5). Perhaps you are a new convert and need to immerse yourself in the life of the church for a period of time before pursuing this goal (3:6). Perhaps you need to repair your reputation in the community before you can move in this direction (3:7). Perhaps there is a part of you that craves power, and you are drawn to being an elder for unholy reasons (1 Pet. 5:2–3). Other believers who know you and love you can speak truth into your life, pointing out factors that you have missed. They can help you know if it is wise to commit right now to the path outlined in this book.

2. Confirmation—Other Believers Can Say "Go for It!"

By the same token, other believers can serve as precious confirmation of the stirrings you are feeling in your heart. They can say, "Yes! This is how you should invest your time!" They can acknowledge your fit for this role, that you have the raw materials to be an elder someday. If you are having doubts, they can provide the affirmation that you will need to actually start (and continue) the process (2 Tim. 1:3–7).

3. Knowledge—Other Believers Can Teach You Theology and Help You Understand Scripture

Simply put, there are people around you with knowledge of theology and insight into the Bible that you do not have (Rom. 15:14). Why would you not avail yourself of those resources? This book will immerse you in Scripture, and the Holy Spirit will guide you as you seek to craft personal, biblical responses to the questions. But having a group of like-minded brothers around will deepen your answers, alert you to what you miss, and bring clarity to the issue at hand.

4. Wisdom—Other Believers Can Help You Connect Theology to Life

Other believers have knowledge that you lack: not only of God and the Bible but also of sin, people, and life (1 Cor. 11:1; Heb. 13:7). They can help you anticipate and prepare for the practical challenges you will face as an elder. As you walk with others through the questions of this book, the Holy Spirit will work through them to help you make connections between real-life ministry scenarios and biblical principles. The wisdom of others will help you maximize the transformational value of the journey (Prov. 11:14; 19:20).

5. Encouragement—Other Believers Will Cheer You On When You Are Tempted to Give Up

Ultimately, growing in godliness is richly rewarding. But this world, our enemy, and even our flesh fight against us every step of the way. Discouragement, distraction, and defeat are their aims. You need encouragement from other believers to refocus, to keep going, to not give up. Christian community fuels perseverance (Heb. 3:12–13). Others watch out for you (10:24), build you up (1 Thess. 5:11), and ease your burdens (Gal. 6:2). If you want to finish strong, link arms with your brothers. Two or three are better than one (Eccles. 4:9–12).

6. Accountability—Other Believers Can Hold You to Your Commitments

Encouragement and accountability will help you persevere. Encouragement builds you up; accountability holds you fast. And you need both. You need brothers who will look you in the eye and say, "You committed to this. I will not let you quit. You are not giving in to passivity or falling to the wayside—not on my watch! We are going to finish this, together." This is brothers living together in harmony (Ps. 133:1). This is why the writer of Hebrews reminds us to continue meeting together (Heb. 10:25). Find two or three others who can hold you to finishing this book and living the life it engenders, and you also can be that gift to them.

7. Refinement—Other Believers Can Point Out Your Blind Spots and Speak to Your Sin

When you let others close, they see things that you miss. They see habits you justify, good gifts that have become idols, entrenched perspectives that are ignoble, links to this world that must be jettisoned. They see sin that has blinded your eyes and settled in your soul. And God will use them to refine and reshape. Trust us, we know it is not always pleasant! But the wounds of such friends are trustworthy (Prov. 27:6). God's plan is that members of the body of Christ would rebuke one another toward holiness (Prov. 15:31–33; Luke 17:3). If you truly desire the growth God has for you, you will welcome such blows (Ps. 141:5). They will sharpen you (Prov. 27:17), making you a humble overseer of God's house (1 Pet. 5:3).

8. Motivation—Other Believers Can Inspire You to Pursue Godliness and Righteousness

There are ungodly motivations for aspiring to be an elder: unwilling obligation, greed, or desire for power (1 Pet. 5:2–3). But there are godly motivations as well—and emulating people who honor Christ is one of them. Timothy was told to look at Paul and follow his teaching (2 Tim. 3:10). The Corinthian church likewise was told to imitate Paul (1 Cor. 4:16; 11:1). Godly leaders—and even children—provide examples to us (Matt. 18:2–5; 1 Tim. 4:12; Heb. 13:7). The saints of old are witnesses to the life of faith (Heb. 12:1). Such people can inspire from afar, but the substance of their faith—and the motivation for spiritual growth—is maximized when you are in close relationship. Seeing their life and habits up close will fuel your passion for sanctification.

This motivation can come from godly mentors, but it can also come from peers. If you pursue this book with two other men and see them becoming more like Ezra—growing in knowledge, in obedience, in ability to teach—you will put your hand to the plow and not look back (Luke 9:62). And they will be inspired by the work of the Holy Spirit in you.

People can motivate you in other ways. Consider how such a journey will bless your wife, strengthen your marriage, and undergird your children's faith. Consider how your friends will be encouraged that growth is possible! Your coworkers will sense the increased fragrance of Christ; your neighbors will see your good works. Reflecting on the blessing that this will be to your family, your community, and your church will likewise motivate you to finish the race.

9. Celebration—Other Believers Can Join You in Praising God for the Work He Is Doing in You

Celebrating is close to the heart of God (Luke 15:6, 10, 22–25, 32). The work he does in his people by his Spirit is constantly acknowledged and celebrated in the Epistles and the letters to the churches in Revelation (1 Cor. 1:4–9; Eph. 1:15–17; Phil. 1:3–5; 2 Tim. 1:3–5; 2 John 1:4; Rev. 2:2–3, 13, 19; 3:8–11). And the final image in heaven is one of feasting, delight, and unending joy (Rev. 5:9–14; 19:5–8). On earth, we taste this joy through other believers. As God works among people in fellowship, and as his transforming power is displayed for all to see, he receives glory and praise.

If you go through this book alone, others will eventually see your progress. But the degree of shared celebration will be minimal. Others will miss your small victories. Few will register your diligence. Your steady faithfulness will go unnoticed. And opportunities to give God glory will be lost. In contrast, if you go through this book with a cohort of like-minded brothers, praise will constantly be on all of your lips; you will exalt his name together (Ps. 34:1–3). This will fuel your growth and magnify our King.

10. Prayer—Other Believers Can Pray for You, Inviting God's Power, Protection, and Provision for Your Growth

We have saved the most central and perhaps most obvious benefit of Christian community for last: prayer. Oh, what a blessing is prayer! How precious, how valuable, how essential. When you walk through this book having enlisted prayer from your spouse, from your pastor, from your peers, you will be protected from attack, you will find strength to overcome, and you will find zeal to engage and power to persevere. Without prayer, don't expect much. As sincere as your desire is, and even as valuable as time alone with God's Word will be, the growth will be slow and intermittent compared to what it would be with earnest, fervent, faithful prayer offered up for you by other believers.

God commands his people to pray for one another (Eph. 6:18; James 5:16); Paul models this (Eph. 1:16–19; Phil. 1:9–11; Col. 1:9), and he asks for prayer himself (Rom. 15:30; Col. 4:3; Eph. 6:19–20; 1 Thess. 5:25; 2 Thess. 3:1). The sense from Scripture is that those who pray for others bolster their faith and propel their growth. Consider the way Paul describes Epaphras in Colossians 4:12–13:

Epaphras, who is one of you, a servant of Christ Jesus, sends you greetings. He is always wrestling for you in his prayers, so that you can stand mature and fully assured in everything God wills. For I testify about him that he works hard for you, for those in Laodicea, and for those in Hierapolis. (CSB)

Don't you want such support as you grow toward being an elder? Enlist such people to pray for you. The value will be incalculable.

Gather a Team

In light of all this, we again urge you: do not go through this book alone. If you are an individual who longs to grow toward being an elder, receive this encouragement.[1]

First, if you are married, talk with your wife. Share the vision of this book with her, consider the time that will be necessary to embrace the work, evaluate your schedule, and dream together about the value this will have for your life and your family. Ask for her prayer support and her sincere partnership in this journey. Ask if she has any concerns, and seek deep spiritual unity in this decision. If you have children of an appropriate age, it would be wise to explain this vision to them and ask for their prayers.

Second, talk to your pastor and church leadership. If you do not have a church or do not know the leadership at all, please do not pursue the path outlined in this book yet. Invest yourself in a church. Serve and pray for the leadership, seek their confirmation of your call, enlist their prayer support, and ask for their involvement in this journey. It would be ideal if a pastor, an elder, or a respected layperson could walk through this process with you and your group (see below).

---

1. If you are a pastor and seek to proactively grow a group of future elders, we encourage you to lay the suggestions in this section before those you seek to grow. We speak more about this in chapter 5.

Third, seek at least two or three others who will join you in working through the book.[2] Commit to meet weekly to discuss and refine your answers, pray for one another, and grow in godliness together. This community will maximize the value of this process and have the added benefit of multiplying those who will (Lord willing) be equipped to be overseers of God's flock.

Making a Choice

If you are in Christ, you are on a trajectory toward glory. God saved you to conform you to the image of his Son (Rom. 8:29–30), which is happening now and will be complete when you see Christ face-to-face (1 John 3:2). Yet growth is often slow, and we are often mired in the status quo. This book is an invitation to make progress by making a choice. Choose to pursue godly character by immersing yourself in God's Word; choose to prepare yourself for service by contemplating the needs of the church; and choose to maximize the process by engaging the community of God's people around you. If God is calling you to do this, do not do it alone.

2. If you wonder about who you would ask to join you on this journey, please read chapter 5 for wisdom on recruitment.

5

Identifying Potential Elders

And what you have heard from me in the presence of many witnesses entrust to faithful men, who will be able to teach others also.

2 Timothy 2:2

First Timothy 3 and Titus 1 spell out lofty qualifications for elders. Elders must be above reproach in character, have a commendable track record at home and in the community, and be able to handle the Word of God as both an offensive and defensive weapon. We agree with those who reason from Scripture that elders should be male.[1]

But it is worth remembering that those whom you recruit for this training process could be younger, still maturing in faith and knowledge,

1. See Alexander Strauch, *Biblical Eldership: An Urgent Call to Restore Biblical Church Leadership*, 2nd ed. (Littleton, CO: Lewis and Roth, 1995); Benjamin Merkle, *40 Questions about Elders and Deacons* (Grand Rapids: Kregel, 2008); and Jeramie Rinne, *Church Elders: How to Shepherd God's People Like Jesus*, 9Marks (Wheaton: Crossway, 2014).

still discerning their own spiritual gift pattern, still acquiring a reputation for being above reproach, and still establishing a track record. They may not have a wife who can testify to their character or children whose lives display their ability to lead by precept and example. So the process of recruiting someone to be trained is slightly different from recruiting an elder.

Your aim as a pastor or serving elder is to discern who within the fellowship might be a potential elder at some point in the future, someone who could be challenged now to submit to a training regimen that will by its very nature help you, fellow elders, and the trainee discern if the congregation (or present elders, if that is your church polity) should invite him to prayerfully consider serving in that role. After this discernment process, you must seek to answer two questions. First, what are the qualities you want to look for in those you invite to be trained? Second, what process should you follow to discern who these men are and to actually recruit them?

Some Qualities to Look For

Here are the qualities we suggest you try to discern, listed in an order of increasing visibility. First, as far as you can discern it, those you recruit should have *rightly ordered loves*. They love God wholeheartedly (Deut. 6:5; Matt. 22:37), and it shows in their obedience to him (Deut. 11:13). They love God's Word (Ps. 119:97). They genuinely love God's people (Rom. 12:9–10). Because God loved them when they were far off, they love the stranger (Deut. 10:18–19). The married man loves his wife sacrificially (Eph. 5:25–33); the single man will already be a one-woman kind of man. Because of what they *do* love, they *do not* love money (1 Tim. 6:10), nor the world (as Demas did; 2 Tim. 4:10), nor the things in the world (1 John 2:15).

Second, they are *faithful*. Second Timothy 2:2 specifies this as an indispensable trait of those to whom we are to entrust the gospel that we have received. This is the quality that Jesus will reward in his servants and stewards of the Word when he returns (Matt. 24:45–46; 1 Cor. 4:2–5). Peter noted this quality in Silvanus, who served as his amanuensis or scribe (1 Pet. 5:12). That should be a reminder that faithfulness in little things is key (Luke 16:10; 19:17). Nehemiah, whose leadership was exemplary, certainly took this into account when he gave Hananiah, governor of the fortress, charge over Jerusalem, "for he was a more faithful and God-fearing man than many" (Neh. 7:2). Hananiah, like Nehemiah's brother Hanani, had a track record of handling responsibility well.

Third, recruit men who are *able*. Scripture makes this distinction, and we should not shrink from doing so. There are people who have a wonderful heart for the Lord and his Word and work, who love what they should and don't love what they shouldn't, but who don't manifest competence. The church needs able elders. It may not be obvious at an early stage in someone's growth and training, but often leaders can already tell who is able to get things done and who is not. When Joseph was resettling his brothers in Egypt, he took five—not eleven—of his brothers in to meet Pharaoh. That already implies some selectivity. Pharaoh let them settle in Goshen and said to Joseph, "If you know any able men among them, put them in charge of my livestock" (Gen. 47:6). What Pharaoh wanted for his flock, God wants for his: able men. The competencies can vary widely, and they should; elders are not to be clones of the pastor, but all elders are to be able to teach (1 Tim. 3:2). Elders will also have a range of other abilities; they should not be mere passengers who are unable to shoulder meaningful responsibility.

Aspects of Discernment

How, then, do we discern who we should ask to join this training process, and how do we ask? I (Greg) have already borne witness to how I stumbled into this, so let me now tell you what I think is genuinely transferable to your situation, whatever it is.

Pray. This is the inviolable rule in all God-honoring recruiting in the local church. We can learn from the church's first leadership selection decision, recorded in Acts 1. When the apostles became convinced through prayer that Scripture mandated that they seek a replacement for Judas Iscariot (Acts 1:14–20), they spelled out the basic requirements of the position and set forth two candidates who, as far as they could see, were qualified (1:21–23). Then they prayed to God, the heart-knower, to guide them to make the right decision (1:24). Pray that God will lead you to those whom you should ask to join this training process. Keep praying this as you observe potential aspiring elders.

Watch. Keep your eyes peeled for faithful, God-loving servants of the church. You may see them in a Bible study, but you may also see them serving in some other capacity. Do not rely only on your observations; consult others. They may see potential that you do not see. Paul did not consider John Mark faithful, but Barnabas saw potential in him (Acts 15:36–41).

Challenge. Help emerging leaders establish a track record of faithfulness by steering them toward responsibilities for which they seem gifted and suited in other ways, tasks at which they are likely to succeed as they walk by faith in obedience. Don't give a massive assignment to a beginner. Any task, when done as to the Lord, can be meaningful. The outcome, whatever it is, will be instructive for them and for you. A successful class or Bible study or outreach will encourage them and you. Someone who is unwilling to take on a modest assignment may not be elder material. When it comes to lowly assignments, remember Jesus's example in washing his disciples' feet, which comes with an explicit command to follow his example (John 13:13–17).

Discern. Look for sacrificial love for people and the church. Paul could say of Timothy, "For I have no one like him, who will be genuinely concerned for your welfare. For they all seek their own interests, not those of Jesus Christ. But you know Timothy's proven worth, how as a son with a father he has served with me in the gospel" (Phil.

2:20–22). Paul relied on Timothy's public track record to predict how he would serve the church. Many potential trainees will already have a solid track record of service to the church or some other ministry. Don't neglect the already-mature believer. On the other hand, don't assume that someone who can lead in some other sphere in the community is qualified to be an elder.

Listen. Make the most of conversations. Listen for clues that God has implanted in someone an aspiration to become qualified for the noble task of being an overseer of his church (1 Tim. 3:1). For those of us who preach, listening is sometimes the most difficult assignment. For the leader at every level, it is usually the best use of our time. Do you recall how the crew of that storm-tossed ship knew that the tempest was related to Jonah? "Then the men were seized by a great fear and said to him, 'What is this you've done?' The men knew he was fleeing from the LORD's presence *because he had told them*" (Jon. 1:10 CSB, emphasis added). People will tell you what is really going on in their lives if you are willing to listen.

The Recruiting Process

How should you go about actually inviting prospective trainees to join this process? You will do this in ways that are in keeping with your personality and with your relationships with the men involved, but here are a few guidelines that may help.

First, start a prayer list of prospective trainees based on what you have heard and seen. As you pray about whether to ask them to train, the Lord will provide the green light, and then the occasion and the right approach.

Second—and this is crucial—when you do speak to them, don't downplay the investment they will have to make in the training; spell it out so that they can count the cost. Make clear to them what they are committing to do and what you are committing to, as well as what the church is *not* committing to. You are not gathering a group of favorites who will automatically be selected to serve as elders. They are not checking off a prerequisite for service, or seeking to gain recognition. Together you are seeking God's face to make you more into the image of Jesus so you can all serve his church more effectively in ways that he directs.

Third, involve each married candidate's wife in the process as early as possible. She needs to be part of the decision. Her prayerful support is vital.

Fourth, expect some men to turn you down. This is not necessarily an indication that they don't have what it takes to serve as an elder; it may in fact indicate that they are wise and judicious. There may be a time later when they will sign on and be eager to join the training process.

Fifth, make the recruiting process communal, just as the training will be. As I recounted earlier, I did this by means of a dessert evening my wife and I hosted for potential trainees and their wives. As you have already read, we think the corporate dimension is vital, so it is best to begin as you intend to continue. Making this a group event communicates that you are all in this together.

Sixth, give people time to think and pray about this so that they do not enter into the training lightly. You don't want them to drop out because they failed to count the cost. That only discourages others and may cause a stampede! Some of that is probably inevitable when reality sets in, but you want to minimize dropouts. You want trainees to persevere, so set them up to succeed, not to fail.

Seventh, be gracious when someone elects not to join the process at this time. The spiritual exercise of seeking God's face will have been good for them, so this does not constitute a failure. Moreover, the size of the trainee group does not matter, unless it is too many to allow real verbal participation. A small group can be excellent.

Eighth, keep a keen eye out for a possible formal or informal co-leader if the group is large enough to call for that. This person's identity may not emerge until the training is underway. That is what happened in my case. But because you are constantly modeling discipling, you should always be bringing someone along as your successor, someone who might run the next leg of the relay race.

Ninth, listen to those you are recruiting. If a different time or format or approach would help more of them succeed, see if you can flex enough to incorporate into the training what they suggest. My group met early on a Tuesday morning, because even those who traveled were usually in town on Mondays and could be with us early on Tuesday. For your group, another time may be better, though be considerate of families. That is why we avoided evenings and Saturday mornings. Additionally, if trainees have a need that you have not thought to address in the training, include it in the list of questions and assignments, if possible. Remember, when Timothy returned to Paul with very encouraging news of how the Thessalonians embraced the gospel, Paul nevertheless listened to the report carefully enough to discern the gaps in their knowledge and walk of faith. He then prayerfully sought to meet them to "supply what is lacking in your faith" (1 Thess. 3:10).

Tenth, plan carefully, and pay attention to logistics. This is not the time to stumble organizationally, even if logistics is not your strong suit. I suggest you write and distribute a detailed prospectus that spells out expectations and the curriculum so that prospective trainees can have that ahead of time. Reading it can be a bit daunting, like what some call "syllabus shock" in graduate education, but my experience is that this foresight will have a positive effect on many prospective trainees. They will feel that at last someone is taking seriously their hunger for real equipping. Be sure to include a survey of the key topics discussed in this book, or just give them the book itself. Logistics may include scheduling the time, the room, and providing coffee or some refreshments. All of this depends on your local setting. God will give you wisdom. He loves the church and wants qualified elders to oversee it. He will guide and provide.

PART 2

TRAINING

6

Seventy-Five Questions for New or Prospective Elders

The seventy-five questions in this chapter form the backbone of the process we are proposing to help you develop as an elder. They are designed to help you get into the Bible and discover truths, hone disciplines and ministry practices, and grow in obedience. More than that, they are written with the aim of equipping you to internalize doctrine and gain biblical wisdom that will be evident to those you serve and before whom you model growing Christlikeness. The questions are listed first as a sort of checklist. Although they are numbered sequentially, you may tackle them in any order and at any pace that suits your group. Following the list, we then lay out the questions one by one, with biblical texts[1] and supplemental resources. For some questions, we offer minimal additional guidance; others require more verbiage to be useful. Where deemed appropriate, we list some of the many resources that could

---

1. Our default translation is the ESV. We have pointed to another translation where the wording is particularly helpful.

round out your study and perhaps answer lingering questions. The key thing is to engage the subject prayerfully and wholeheartedly and give undistracted attention to the biblical texts, always reading them in context to discern what each verse is saying and doing. Spend the time necessary to write out observations and answers. This will help fix them in your mind and will also facilitate sharing when your group meets. The value of this book depends largely on how much focused time and energy you invest in using these questions.

1. What does the Bible claim concerning itself?
2. What should a believer's posture toward Scripture be?
3. What does the Bible say about telling the truth?
4. What plan do you follow for personal Bible reading and study?
5. What are basic guidelines for faithful interpretation of the Bible?
6. How does one effectively lead a small-group Bible study?
7. What should we believe and teach about God's triune nature?
8. What are the benefits of memorizing Scripture?
9. What is God like? What are his attributes?
10. What should you do to prepare to read Scripture in public worship?
11. How do you encourage someone in sound doctrine? How do you recognize false doctrine? How do you refute error?
12. How do you make a case for the deity of Christ? Why is it important to affirm that Jesus is fully God?
13. What is the importance of servanthood?
14. How can Jesus be both fully human and fully divine yet one person?
15. What does the Lord's Prayer teach us about prayer and how we should pray?
16. Why did Jesus die? How do you understand the atonement? What difference does this make in practice?

17. What is the gospel? How do you explain the gospel to unbelievers?

18. Why do you believe that Jesus was raised from the dead? What can be known about his resurrection body?

19. What is included in the present ministry of the ascended Lord Jesus?

20. What does the Bible teach about fasting? How do you practice it?

21. What do we know about Jesus's second coming?

22. How do you describe the person and work of the Holy Spirit? How has the Spirit's ministry changed since Old Testament times?

23. How would you distinguish between the baptism of the Holy Spirit and the fullness of the Holy Spirit?

24. How can someone discover his or her spiritual gifts?

25. What is the place of prayer in the economy of God?

26. How should you lead the congregation in prayer in public worship?

27. How should you offer proactive Christian counsel?

28. How should you comfort the bereaved?

29. What is the human condition apart from Christ? What happens to those who have not heard the gospel when they die? What happens to those who have heard and rejected the gospel?

30. What elements would you include in a three-minute version of your testimony? Write out such a version and be prepared to share it.

31. What must happen for someone to be saved? Address predestination, election, justification, repentance, rebirth, faith, and grace in your answer.

32. What has "taking up your cross" meant to you in practice?

33. What word pictures does the New Testament use to describe the church? What does each picture imply concerning the nature and purpose of the church?

34. What is your attitude toward those in authority in various spheres?

35. How are individuals initiated into the church? How does baptism relate to a person's salvation?

36. How should you disciple an individual?

37. As you understand Scripture, who may be a member of a local church?

38. What do you do to maintain fellowship with other Christians in your own church and other churches?

39. How do you maintain a good reputation with outsiders?

40. What does the New Testament teach about church leadership?

41. What qualities make one an effective leader in the family?

42. What is the nature and function of the Lord's Supper?

43. How do you practice confession?

44. Is it possible for someone who professes faith in Christ to lose his or her salvation? Why or why not?

45. How do you keep a clear conscience?

46. What is the hope of the individual believer?

47. What is your attitude toward work? What biblical texts shape that attitude?

48. How does one pursue holiness?

49. How do you resist sexual temptation?

50. How does legalism differ from gospel obedience?

51. How should you receive criticism?

52. Who is Satan? What do we know about him from Scripture?

53. How do believers confront and defeat the devil?

54. What is your plan to maintain physical fitness?

55. What constitutes heresy? How should church leaders respond to it?

56. What sorts of conflict should you be prepared to encounter in the church? How does a godly leader address conflict?

57. What sorts of strategies should we use to maintain the priority of corporate, public worship?

58. How do you discern the will of God—for your life, for the church, for the world?

59. What is the role of grace in the life of a believer?

60. What should be a Christian's attitude and practice with regard to giving money?

61. How do you preserve your integrity?

62. How do you keep yourself free from the love of money?

63. How do you pursue humility?

64. What does it mean to "live with your [wife] in an understanding way" (1 Pet. 3:7)?

65. What are your personal habits with regard to planning? What biblical principles undergird and shape planning?

66. How can one impart vision?

67. How do you steward your time—your daily calendar, tasks, rhythms, and year?

68. What should you keep in mind when leading any kind of church meeting, whether a meeting of a board, committee, task force, or the whole congregation?

69. What do you do to control your tongue?

70. How do you deal with emotional or behavioral issues as you pursue transparent godliness?

71. How do you maintain healthy friendships?

72. How do you rebuke or admonish people?

73. How do you teach the Bible?

74. How do you nurture your children for Christ?

75. How would you articulate a robust Christian worldview?

1. What does the Bible claim concerning itself?

Study the following passages in context and draw some conclusions you can defend. Some texts speak to the question directly; others fill in the picture. Notice especially what Scripture claims to be, say, and do.

(1) 2 Timothy 3:14–17; (2) 2 Peter 1:19–21; (3) John 14:26; 16:13; (4) 2 Peter 3:15–16; (5) Hebrews 1:1–2; (6) Titus 1:1–3; (7) John 17:17; (8) 2 Samuel 22:31; (9) Psalm 12:6; (10) Isaiah 40:8; (11) Matthew 24:35; (12) Psalm 138:2; (13) Galatians 3:8; cf. Genesis 12:1–3; (14) Romans 9:17; Exodus 9:16; (15) Hebrews 3:7; Psalm 95:7; (16) John 10:35; (17) Matthew 5:17–18; (18) Psalm 33:4, 6, 9, 11; (19) Hebrews 4:12; (20) 1 Thessalonians 2:13; (21) Isaiah 55:10–11; (22) Romans 3:19–21; (23) Deuteronomy 29:29

Resources

The following supplementary resources may be consulted after you have done your own study of the biblical texts. They are listed beginning with some more basic sources and then more nuanced or advanced ones.

Gregg R. Allison, *Historical Theology*, 37–184
Wayne Grudem, *Bible Doctrine*, 33–49
Wayne Grudem, *Systematic Theology*, 47–138
Michael Horton, *The Christian Faith*, 115–85
Gregory Strand and William Kynes, *Evangelical Convictions*, 51–68

See also these more advanced resources:

Craig L. Blomberg, *Can We Still Believe the Bible?*
D. A. Carson, ed., *The Enduring Authority of the Christian Scriptures*
D. A. Carson and John Woodbridge, eds., *Scripture and Truth*
"Chicago Statement on Biblical Inerrancy"

2. What should a believer's posture toward Scripture be?

It is one thing to acknowledge the truth of what the Bible claims for itself; it is another to maintain a biblical posture toward it. Read the following texts submissively, and ask the Lord to conform your thinking and practice toward what these texts call for.

(1) Psalm 119:16, 18, 24, 30, 35, 40, 42–43, 45, 47–48, 66, 71–72, 74, 77, 81–82, 92–94, 97, 103, 113, 119, 127–29, 140, 143, 147, 159, 161–63, 165, 167;[2] (2) Matthew 5:17–20; (3) John 14:15, 21, 23–24; (4) John 8:55; 10:35

Resources

Kevin DeYoung, *Taking God at His Word*
Timothy Ward, *Words of Life*
Christopher J. H. Wright, *Life through God's Word*

3. What does the Bible say about telling the truth?

Where is truth telling rooted?

(1) Deuteronomy 32:4; (2) 2 Samuel 7:28; (3) Psalm 146:6; (4) Romans 3:4; (5) Titus 1:2; (6) Hebrews 6:18; (7) John 1:14; 14:6; 18:37

Why is telling the truth so important? Notice carefully the context of each text.

(1) Proverbs 12:19; (2) Zephaniah 3:13; (3) Zechariah 8:16; (4) Malachi 2:6; (5) Exodus 20:16

Notice the seriousness of scriptural warnings against lying.

(1) Leviticus 19:11; (2) Psalms 5:6; 63:11; 101:7; (3) Proverbs 12:22; 19:5; 21:6; (4) Colossians 3:9–10; (5) Revelation 21:8

Let the following examples of lying pave the way for self-examination. When are you tempted to lie?

(1) Genesis 3:4; (2) Genesis 4:9; (3) Genesis 27:24

---

2. A useful exercise is to reread the whole of Psalm 119 and notice two things: the many professions of faith in and obedience to God's law, and the many prayers rooted in Scripture and God's character as revealed in it.

What is the biblical standard for speech?

(1) Exodus 18:21; **(2)** Ephesians 4:15, 25; **(3)** Ephesians 6:14; **(4)** 1 Corinthians 5:8; **(5)** Matthew 5:37; **(6)** James 5:12

Resources
Timothy Keller, *Counterfeit Gods*
J. I. Packer, *Keeping the Ten Commandments*, 95–101
Lou Priolo, *Deception*
Colin S. Smith, *The 10 Greatest Struggles of Your Life*, 121–35

4. What plan do you follow for personal Bible reading and study?

Most growing Christians have had more than one strategy for feeding on God's Word. Here are a few of them:

I follow a reading calendar such as the M'Cheyne Reading Plan.

I use a devotional book such as *Daily Light* or *Morning and Evening*.

Like Martin Luther, I read from a book of the Bible until something strikes me.

I receive a verse or passage from an online source and meditate on that.

I read and study passages from which I am preaching or teaching soon.

I read one chapter in the morning and one in the evening.

I read some part of the Bible alone and some portion with my spouse.

My spouse and I read one chapter aloud to each other daily.

I take several hours at once each week to delve into a Bible book.

I use a small-group Bible study guide in connection with a group that meets weekly.

I study passages related to current events or social concerns with which I am grappling.

I meet with someone I am discipling every Saturday morning and we work through a text together.

The options are many. Some people, when forced to be candid, acknowledge that they do not have a disciplined, consistent plan for Bible reading and study. If this describes you, or you are dissatisfied with your current practice, prayerfully consider the following thoughts.

- Hunger for Scripture does not lessen the more you feed on it; the hunger grows.
- Growing Christians should have a strategy to read the whole Bible regularly.
- There is value both in reading larger chunks of Scripture to review the big picture and also in studying smaller portions in depth and detail.
- Variety with respect to the amount of Scripture read or studied can forestall the problems of rushing through one's daily reading or getting bored with thematically similar texts. To put it differently, it is sometimes valuable to vary the pace at which you read.
- Devotional reading of Scripture and exegesis for teaching and preaching are not the same, and one should not be substituted for the other; instead, they complement and enhance each other.
- Hearing without heeding is ultimately counterproductive.
- Auditory learners can get substantial value from listening to Scripture. However, this method can hinder the ability to stop and ponder or explore along the way.
- A realistic plan that actually gets you into the Word and gets the Word into you is better than an impressively ambitious plan that you follow for a few weeks and then abandon.
- Devotional reading should be at a time of day when you are at your best.

- Far from taking away time, committing to prioritizing Bible reading can be part of an ordered, fruitful life where God goes before you, opens and closes doors, and multiplies your time.
- Everyone should expect there to be times when maintaining a vibrant devotional life is more of a struggle than at other times. Practices that seemed to facilitate devotion at one time may not work so well at another time.
- Some sort of "soft accountability" helps some people establish a disciplined pattern of reading and study.

In light of these observations, try to devise a plan for yourself that

builds in variety,

takes you through the whole Bible every year,

allows you to get back on schedule fairly easily,

has some solo reading and some family (or spousal) reading, and

takes into account the way or ways that you learn best.

Evaluation and concrete next steps:

My current plan is . . .

My plan for the next six weeks is . . .

My strategy for soft accountability is . . .

Resources

D. A. Carson, *For the Love of God*
Oswald Chambers, *My Utmost for His Highest*
Paul David Tripp, *New Morning Mercies*

5. What are basic guidelines for faithful interpretation of the Bible?

Sadly, you probably won't serve long as an elder before you learn of a parishioner who holds an unorthodox belief while simultaneously holding the Scriptures in high esteem. The problem could spring from more than one source, but a faulty hermeneutic or reading strategy is often to blame. We list some basic guidelines in "Before You Begin: Steps in Bible Study," in chapter 7. If you have already used that material, see how many of them you can write down. If not, feel free to review them now.

This exercise will attempt to equip you to practice sound biblical interpretation and to help someone else do the same.

What seems to be the problem?

> **(1)** Matthew 22:23–33; **(2)** 2 Peter 3:16b; **(3)** Romans 1:18–32; **(4)** John 5:39–40

Recall a personal example of a word or statement taken out of context to illustrate how important context is.

Steps toward a solution:

> **(1)** Deuteronomy 5:27; **(2)** Deuteronomy 27:9–10; **(3)** Proverbs 1:5; **(4)** Psalm 119:18; **(5)** Deuteronomy 17:19–20; **(6)** Nehemiah 8:8

Devise an exercise in observation of 1 John 3:1–3 to underscore how we don't always see what is there at first glance.

See how many different parts of speech you can identify in the same passage. Distinguish between independent and dependent clauses. Distinguish between clear statements and inferences from what is stated.

What role does this paragraph play in the context? How does a letter such as 1 John communicate in ways that, say, an apocalyptic or poetic passage would not, and vice versa?

Share with your group things you learned or still wonder about from this passage.

Resources

Gordon D. Fee and Douglas Stuart, *How to Read the Bible for All Its Worth*
Walter C. Kaiser Jr. and Moisés Silva, *Introduction to Biblical Hermeneutics*
William W. Klein, Craig L. Blomberg, and Robert L. Hubbard Jr., *Introduction to Biblical Interpretation*

6. How does one effectively lead a small-group Bible study?

The resources listed at the end of this question are exceptional and provide clear summaries of the many issues to consider when leading a small group. Elders have the additional challenge of being looked to as an authority on the text being studied. This is even more the case with the pastor, especially when the text has been or will be the basis of a sermon. There is nothing wrong with knowing the passage thoroughly; indeed, don't attempt to lead a small-group Bible study until you do. The problem arises when you let the group make you the "answer man" in a way that short-circuits the process. Instead, your goal is for every member of the group to look at the passage carefully, interpret it properly, and apply it appropriately. To that end, I (Greg) gradually learned to have many more questions ready than I thought I would need. I resolved never to answer the questions. I lobbed them out and let them sit. I deflected group members' questions to the rest of the group. I sat right beside the quick-to-answer person and used eye contact to encourage others to speak.

After many years of leading small-group Bible studies as a pastor, I began to teach preaching. In preparing for that role, I distilled the process of interrogating a biblical text to six questions, which I had gleaned from various sources. In recent years, I have used these to teach Bible-study methods for small-group leaders, convinced as I am that good answers to these questions maximize faithfulness to texts of any genre.

1. What is this text functionally? That is, is it a command, an explanation, a rebuke, an encouragement, some combination of these, or something else?

2. What is the main subject of this text? Not all the ideas in a passage are the dominant idea; what is it here?

3. What is the passage saying about the subject? If you have rightly identified the main thing a text is speaking about, most other things in it should relate to that idea in some discernable way.

4. What response does this text call for? This naturally relates to the first questions since, for instance, a rebuke calls for repentance and an explanation calls for understanding.

5. How does this text elicit that response? It is tempting to come up with an application that has nothing to do with what the Holy Spirit is using this passage to bring about. The best studies—and sermons—let the text itself do the work of defining the response and beginning to achieve it.

6. How does this text fit into the larger picture, the drama of redemption? Is there an evident connection to Jesus? The key thing is to discern what that is and help your group members discover it.

The best training for leading a small group is to watch someone who is a master of it and then use and adapt their best practices.

Resources
Bill Donahue, *Leading Life-Changing Small Groups*
Greg Scharf, *Let the Earth Hear His Voice*, 110–21
Oletta Wald, *The New Joy of Discovery in Bible Study*

7. What should we believe and teach about God's triune nature?

The doctrine of the Trinity is an attempt to circumscribe and safeguard a mystery—namely, that God is one, yet the Father, the Lord Jesus, and the Holy Spirit are also distinct persons, not less than God.

God is one, and there is no other God.

(1) Deuteronomy 6:4–5; Mark 12:29–30; **(2)** Isaiah 44:6–8; 45:5–7, 14, 18, 22–23; **(3)** 1 Corinthians 8:4; **(4)** Ephesians 4:6; **(5)** 1 Timothy 2:5

Jesus is fully God.

(1) John 1:1–3, 18; **(2)** John 20:28; **(3)** Acts 20:28;[3] **(4)** Romans 9:5; **(5)** Titus 2:13; **(6)** Psalm 45:6–7; Hebrews 1:8–9; **(7)** 2 Peter 1:1; **(8)** 1 John 5:20; **(9)** Revelation 1:8[4]

The Holy Spirit is God.

(1) Acts 5:3–4; **(2)** 2 Corinthians 3:17

Some Old Testament texts hint at the plurality of persons in the Godhead.

(1) Genesis 1:26; 3:22; 11:7; 22:11–18; 32:24–30; **(2)** Exodus 3:2–6; 23:20–22; **(3)** Psalm 110;[5] **(4)** Isaiah 6:8; **(5)** Zechariah 3:1–4

It may be helpful to put texts that speak of the triunity of God in four categories:

1. Clear statements

(a) Matthew 28:19; **(b)** 2 Corinthians 13:14

3. Whose blood?

4. Not all would agree this refers to Jesus, but Revelation 22:13 uses the same title, and in the context (cf. 22:16) it is Jesus who is speaking.

5. This should be understood especially in light of its frequent citation in the New Testament (Matt. 22:44; 26:64; Mark 12:36; 14:62; Luke 20:42–43; 22:69; Acts 2:34–35; Heb. 1:13; 5:6; 7:17, 21).

2. Triadic forms

    (a) Ephesians 4:4–6; **(b)** 1 Corinthians 12:4–6; **(c)** 1 Peter 1:2; **(d)** Ephesians 1:3–14

3. Passages that mention the three persons together but do not specifically describe their relationship

    (a) Galatians 4:4–6; **(b)** Mark 1:9–11; **(c)** Acts 1:4–5; **(d)** Romans 5:5–6; **(e)** Romans 8:1–4; **(f)** 2 Thessalonians 2:13–14; **(g)** Titus 3:4–6; **(h)** Jude 20–21

4. Passages that describe some facet of the relationship between persons of the Godhead

    (a) John 5:26; 14:6; **(b)** John 15:26; 16:15; 17:20–24

Consider the impact of this truth and these texts on prayer (Eph. 2:18; Rom. 8:26–27) and on evangelism (Eph. 1:3–14), especially when interacting with Jehovah's Witnesses (John 1:1, 18) and Oneness Pentecostals.

Resources

Gregg R. Allison, *Historical Theology*, 231–53
Wayne Grudem, *Bible Doctrine*, 104–23
Michael Horton, *The Christian Faith*, 273–306
J. I. Packer, *Concise Theology*, 40–42
Fred Sanders, *The Deep Things of God*
Robert Shaw, *The Reformed Faith*, 71–78
Gregory Strand and William Kynes, *Evangelical Convictions*, 41–44

8. What are the benefits of memorizing Scripture?

(1) Psalm 119:11; **(2)** Deuteronomy 6:6–9, 12; **(3)** Deuteronomy 11:18–23; **(4)** Joshua 1:8; **(5)** Psalm 37:31; **(6)** Psalm 40:8; **(7)** Jeremiah 31:33–34; Hebrews 8:10; 10:16; **(8)** Jeremiah 32:40; **(9)** Colossians 3:16; **(10)** Matthew 4:1–11

How can one memorize Scripture? This will depend on your learning style, age, and other factors. It usually helps to memorize in the translation you find most suitable. You may also find the following suggestions helpful.

1. Read it repeatedly.
2. Speak it aloud.
3. Write it out.
4. Place it where you will see it often.
5. Listen to it.
6. Sing it.
7. Share it: recite it for the edification of others.

Resources

Joshua Choonmin Kang, *Scripture by Heart*
The Navigators, *Topical Memory System*
There are also many helpful Bible memorization apps.

9. What is God like? What are his attributes?

It is always a good practice when studying any passage of Scripture to ask what it teaches about God. Here are some passages where the answer to that question should be fairly easy to discern. Theologians often distinguish God's incommunicable attributes—how he differs from us—from his communicable attributes—how we are like him.[6] In these passages, try to find at least ten attributes of God and be ready to briefly define each.

(1) Acts 17:24–25; (2) Psalm 90:2; (3) Isaiah 43:7; (4) Psalm 102:25–27; (5) Genesis 1:1; John 1:3; (6) Jeremiah 23:23–24; Psalm 139:7–10; (7) John 4:24; (8) John 1:18; 1 Timothy 6:16; 1 John 4:12; (9) Romans 16:27; 11:33; (10) Deuteronomy 32:4; Titus 1:2; (11) Luke 18:19; Psalm 34:8; (12) 1 John 4:8; Romans 5:8; (13) Exodus 34:6; Psalm 103:8; 2 Samuel 24:14; Romans 3:23–24; (14) Psalm 71:22; Isaiah 6:3; Psalm 99:9; (15) Deuteronomy 32:4; Genesis 18:25; (16) Isaiah 48:11; (17) Deuteronomy 9:7–8; Romans 1:18; 1 Thessalonians 1:10; (18) Psalm 115:3; Daniel 4:35; (19) Jeremiah 32:17, 27; Ephesians 3:20; Matthew 19:26; (20) Matthew 5:48; (21) 1 Timothy 6:15; (22) Psalm 27:4; (23) Hebrews 1:3

6. The texts listed here are some of those that Wayne Grudem lists on pages 160–225 of *Systematic Theology*, roughly in the order he lists them, beginning with the texts that relate to the attributes that are true of God alone.

What attributes of God comfort and encourage you the most?

Which do you find most difficult to explain?

Resources
Wayne Grudem, *Bible Doctrine*, 67–103
Wayne Grudem, *Systematic Theology*, chaps. 11–13
Mark Jones, *God Is*
J. I. Packer, *Concise Theology*, 16–61
A. W. Tozer, *The Knowledge of the Holy*

10. What should you do to prepare to read Scripture in public worship?

(1) 1 Timothy 4:12–16

It may help to review some of these verses for attitudinal preparation and to pray for those who read Scripture in public.

(1) Psalm 1:1–3; **(2)** 2 Timothy 3:14–17; **(3)** Psalm 119:17–20; **(4)** Nehemiah 8:1–8; **(5)** 2 Kings 22:8–13; **(6)** Colossians 3:12–17; **(7)** Isaiah 55:8–11; **(8)** Hebrews 4:12; **(9)** Isaiah 66:1–2; **(10)** Deuteronomy 30:11–14; **(11)** Romans 12:1–2; **(12)** Matthew 4:4

Here are some reminders about the technical side of public reading:

- *Listen to it.* It's wise to go online and hear how a vocal professional reads the passage, especially if there are unfamiliar names or places.
- *Understand it.* Meditate on the passage until its truth and beauty are clear to you. Your reading should not sound like you are reading. Just say what the text is saying using the very words of the text. The text conveys meaning. Until you know the meaning of the passage, you will not be able to read it effectively. For instance, pronouns are not normally emphasized. They stand for their antecedents; the verbs associated

with them are often what is intended to add to the meaning of the text.

- *Practice it.* Read the passage aloud at least eight times from the copy of the Bible you will use in the worship service. Lightly mark your Bible in pencil to remind you of pauses, emphases, and other things you have discovered while practicing. (Some recommend printing the text and marking that. This has advantages, but the visual reinforcement for congregants of seeing someone read from what is obviously a Bible outweighs this.) Project your voice and slightly overarticulate, because some clarity is inevitably lost between your mouth and your listeners' ears.

- *Pray about it.* Ask the God of truth to speak the truth of his Word through his words to his people.

- *Do not be dramatic.* Dramatic reading only calls attention to yourself as reader. For the same reason, don't greet the congregation when you stand to read; merely invite them to turn to the passage and follow along as you read. Avoid the instruction, "Read with me," which is ambiguous. Worshipers will not know whether to vocalize or listen silently.

Resources

Jeffrey Arthurs, *Devote Yourself to the Public Reading of Scripture*
Max McLean, *Unleashing the Word*
Thomas Edward McComiskey, *Reading Scripture in Public*

---

11. How do you encourage someone in sound doctrine? How do you recognize false doctrine? How do you refute error?

(1) Titus 1:9; **(2)** 2 Timothy 3:14–17; **(3)** Psalm 25:4–5; **(4)** 1 Timothy 4:6–16; **(5)** 2 Timothy 2:14–15; **(6)** Titus 3:4–9; **(7)** Acts 17:11; **(8)** 1 John 4:2–3; **(9)** 2 Timothy 4:3–4; **(10)** 2 Peter 2:1–3; **(11)** Titus 2:1; **(12)** Mark 12:24–27; **(13)** Acts 18:24–26; **(14)** Galatians 2:11–16; **(15)** Ephesians 4:11–16; 5:6–11; **(16)** 2 Timothy 2:23–26; 4:2; **(17)** James 1:19–21; 5:19–20; **(18)** 2 Peter 3:17–18

As you reflect on the need for elders to defend sound doctrine and refute error, consider the suggestions below.

Know sound doctrine.
- Read and reread the Bible.
- Read the creeds.
- Read systematic theology. There is a pattern to sound doctrine.
- Identify central truths and secondary issues.

Recognize patterns of false doctrine.
- Truth denied
- Truth supplemented in a way that denies the sufficiency of the gospel
- Truth neglected
- Truth misapplied
- Truth out of proportion

Defend sound doctrine.
- Overcome lies by truth, distortion by proportion, and neglect by emphasis.
- Teach the truth.
- Ask questions, listen, and seek to understand.
- Look for patterns of false doctrine.
- Look together to the Scriptures in context.
- Speak the truth in love.
- Admonish those in error.
- If the error remains, take appropriate steps to protect the church.

Resources

Justin S. Holcomb, *Know the Heretics*
Bobby Jamieson, *Sound Doctrine*
Jonathan Leeman, *Church Discipline*

12. How do you make a case for the deity of Christ? Why is it important to affirm that Jesus is fully God?

(1) John 1:1–3, 18; **(2)** John 20:28; **(3)** Acts 20:28;[7] **(4)** Romans 9:5; **(5)** Titus 2:13; **(6)** Psalm 45:7–8; Hebrews 1:8–9; **(7)** 2 Peter 1:1; **(8)** 1 John 5:20; **(9)** Revelation 1:8

See also:

(10) Philippians 2:6 (CSB); **(11)** Colossians 2:9 (CSB); **(12)** John 14:9; **(13)** John 8:46; **(14)** 2 Corinthians 5:21; **(15)** 1 Peter 2:22; **(16)** 1 John 3:5

Resources

Bruce Demarest, *Who Is Jesus?*
Wayne Grudem, *Bible Doctrine*, 229–47
Murray J. Harris, *Jesus as God*
Gregory Strand and William Kynes, *Evangelical Convictions*, 93–96

13. What is the importance of servanthood?

The following texts are grouped to underscore various facets of biblical teaching on servanthood.

(1) Isaiah 49:5;[8] **(2)** Isaiah 52:13; **(3)** Isaiah 53:11; **(4)** Mark 10:45; **(5)** Luke 12:37; **(6)** Revelation 1:6; 5:10 (NIV); **(7)** Luke 4:8; **(8)** Luke 16:13; **(9)** 1 Thessalonians 1:9; **(10)** 1 Peter 5:2 (NIV); **(11)** Ephesians 6:7; **(12)** Romans 1:9; 12:7; **(13)** Galatians 5:13; **(14)** 1 Timothy 6:2; **(15)** 1 Timothy 3:10; **(16)** 1 Peter 4:10; **(17)** Revelation 22:3

Resources

Duane Elmer, *Cross-Cultural Servanthood*
Nate Palmer, *Servanthood as Worship*

7. Whose blood?
8. The Isaiah texts are drawn from the Servant Songs and are messianic, so Jesus exemplifies these perfectly.

14. How can Jesus be both fully human and fully divine yet one person?

If you are working through these questions out of order, make sure you answer question 12 before tackling this one.

(1) 1 John 4:2–3; **(2)** 2 John 7; **(3)** Matthew 4:2; **(4)** John 4:6; **(5)** Luke 8:45–47; **(6)** John 11:35, 38; **(7)** Mark 13:32; **(8)** Mark 14:32–42; **(9)** Luke 12:50; **(10)** Hebrews 5:7–10; **(11)** Hebrews 2:17–18; 4:15–16; 5:2, 7–9

It took some time before Christians could clearly say that the eternal Word, the Second Person of the Trinity, after his incarnation, was one person, the God-man, to whom both divine and human attributes could be properly attributed. Some of the missteps along the way included Docetism, Gnosticism, Ebionism, Arianism, Modalism (also called Sabellianism), Apollinarianism, Nestorianism, and Eutychianism. The Allison chapter cited below will give you a clear summary of how these ideas were wide of the mark and how the creeds of Nicaea and Chalcedon countered them.

What difference does it make for everyday Christians that we get this right?

Resources
Gregg R. Allison, *Historical Theology*, 365–88
Wayne Grudem, *Bible Doctrine*, 229–47
J. I. Packer, *Concise Theology*, 108–10
Gregory Strand and William Kynes, *Evangelical Convictions*, 97–100
Stephen J. Wellum, *God the Son Incarnate*

15. What does the Lord's Prayer teach us about prayer and how we should pray?

(1) Matthew 6:5–15; (2) Luke 11:1–13

The Bible is loaded with other texts that teach about prayer by precept and example. As you read these, let them inform practical questions concerning prayer that you may be called on to answer.

(1) Matthew 7:7–11; (2) Luke 22:39–46; (3) Philippians 4:6; (4) 1 Timothy 2:1–7; (5) 1 Thessalonians 5:16–18; (6) Romans 8:26; (7) Luke 18:1–8; (8) 1 John 1:9; (9) 2 Chronicles 6:12–21; Ezra 9:5–15; (10) James 5:13–18; (11) 1 John 5:14–15; (12) Mark 11:22–25; (13) John 14:12–14; (14) Ephesians 6:18; (15) Psalm 32

Resources

Wayne Grudem, *Systematic Theology*, chap. 18
J. I. Packer, *Praying the Lord's Prayer*
R. C. Sproul, *The Prayer of the Lord*
Warren W. Wiersbe, *On Earth as It Is in Heaven*

16. Why did Jesus die? How do you understand the atonement? What difference does this make in practice?

(1) Matthew 27:32–66; (2) John 11:49–52; (3) Habakkuk 1:13; (4) Psalm 5:4–6; (5) Psalm 51:3–5; (6) Romans 1:18; 2:5–9; (7) Romans 3:9–20; (8) Leviticus 16:1–34; (9) Leviticus 23:26–32; (10) Hebrews 9:6–14; 10:1–4; (11) Isaiah 53:4–6; (12) Matthew 20:28; (13) Romans 3:21–26; (14) Romans 4:3–8; (15) Romans 5:6–11; (16) Romans 8:3; (17) Colossians 1:20; 2:11–15; (18) 1 John 2:2; 4:9–10; (19) 2 Corinthians 5:21; (20) Ephesians 1:3–14; (21) Revelation 1:4–6; 5:9–10; (22) 1 Peter 1:18–19; 2:24; (23) Hebrews 9:28; (24) Matthew 26:28; (25) 2 Corinthians 5:14–16; (26) Romans 6; (27) Hebrews 2:14–18; (28) 1 Corinthians 6:20; 7:23

Resources

Gregg R. Allison, *Historical Theology*, 389–410
Bruce Demarest, *The Cross and Salvation*
Michael Horton, *The Christian Faith*, 492–552
J. I. Packer, *Concise Theology*, 134–36

Thomas R. Schreiner, *New Testament Theology*, 265–74, 276–86, 300–303, 364–65, 419, 429–30

John R. W. Stott, *The Cross of Christ*[9]

Gregory Strand and William Kynes, *Evangelical Convictions*, 113–31

17. What is the gospel? How do you explain the gospel to unbelievers?

(1) 1 Corinthians 15:1–4; (2) Isaiah 53:4–6; (3) Romans 1:1–6; (4) Romans 1:16–17; (5) Romans 2:12–16; (6) Romans 3:9–26; (7) Romans 4:5; (8) Romans 6:23; (9) Romans 10:8–13; (10) Ephesians 2:1–10; (11) John 3:16; (12) John 14:6; (13) Titus 3:4–7; (14) 2 Corinthians 5:18–21; (15) 1 John 4:9–10; (16) 1 Peter 2:24; (17) Acts 16:31; (18) Acts 2:36–38

Resources

Mark Dever, *The Gospel and Personal Evangelism*, chaps. 2–5

Greg Gilbert, *What Is the Gospel?*

Wayne Grudem, *Systematic Theology*, chap. 33

Will Metzger, *Tell the Truth*, esp. parts 1 and 2

J. I. Packer, *Evangelism and the Sovereignty of God*, 60–74

18. Why do you believe that Jesus was raised from the dead? What can be known about his resurrection body?

Notice carefully what the gospels affirm happened *before* the resurrection as well as after it.

(1) Matthew 27:45–28:15; (2) Mark 15:33–16:8; (3) Luke 23:44–24:53; (4) John 19:28–20:29

Follow the logic of the resurrection by carefully reading 1 Corinthians 15.

9. Notice especially how Stott underscores four New Testament images that may help you communicate the meaning of the cross: the law court, where a fine is paid; the slave market, where we are bought back; the family, where we are restored to the Father; and the temple, where an atoning sacrifice is offered and accepted.

Use a concordance to discover how prominently Christ's resurrection featured in apostolic preaching.

Notice some implications of the resurrection for the Lord Jesus.

(1) Acts 2:24, 31, 34; (2) 1 Corinthians 15:54–57; (3) Acts 5:31; (4) Acts 13:34, 37; (5) Romans 1:4; (6) Acts 1:9–11; Philippians 2:9–11; (7) Revelation 1:18

Clearly the resurrection of Jesus benefits us believers too. Note some of the benefits from the following texts.

(1) Romans 4:23–25; (2) Romans 8:11; 10:9; (3) Hebrews 7:25; (4) John 6:40, 44, 54; (5) Acts 3:26; 4:10; 10:40; 13:30–39; (6) 1 Corinthians 15:17, 58; (7) John 11:25–26; (8) 1 Thessalonians 4:13–18

What can you conclude from the following texts concerning Jesus's resurrection body?

(1) Luke 24:39; (2) John 20:19–20, 27; (3) Acts 1:3; (4) 1 Corinthians 15:42–46, 52–54; (5) Philippians 3:21; (6) Hebrews 7:16, 24; (7) Romans 6; (8) Ephesians 1:19–2:10; (9) Colossians 2:9–15; 3:1–4[10]

Resources

Gregg R. Allison, *Historical Theology*, 411–29[11]
Michael Horton, *The Christian Faith*, 521–29
J. I. Packer, *Concise Theology*, 125–26
Robert Shaw, *The Reformed Faith*, 371–78
Gregory Strand and William Kynes, *Evangelical Convictions*, 128–30

19. What is included in the present ministry of the ascended Lord Jesus?

(1) Acts 1:7–11; 1 Timothy 3:16; (2) Acts 2:32–36; 7:55–56; (3) Philippians 2:9; (4) Hebrews 1:1–4; 2:9–10; (5) Hebrews 6:19–20; 7:23–28; 10:12–14; (6) 1 John 2:1–2;

10. Note how the Colossians passages draw out implications of our union with Christ in his death and resurrection.
11. This chapter is a helpful review of the history of objections to the resurrection of Jesus.

(7) John 14:2–3; 16:7; **(8)** Ephesians 1:19b–23; 1 Peter 3:22; Psalm 110:1; **(9)** Ephesians 2:6; **(10)** Ephesians 4:7–13; **(11)** Revelation 1:12–18; 5:1–14

Resources

Wayne Grudem, *Systematic Theology*, 617–20
Timothy Keller, *Encountering Jesus*, chap. 9
Jonny Woodrow and Tim Chester, *The Ascension*

20. What does the Bible teach about fasting? How do you practice it?

Recalling that biblical examples may not be normative, look at the following texts and ask the Lord to help you discern how these examples, instructions, and predictions might inform your own practice.

(1) Deuteronomy 9:9; **(2)** Esther 4:15–17; **(3)** Nehemiah 9:1–5; **(4)** Daniel 10:3; **(5)** 2 Chronicles 20:2–4; **(6)** Ezra 8:21–23; **(7)** Joel 1:13–14; 2:12–15; **(8)** Isaiah 58:5–14 (CSB); **(9)** Zechariah 8:18–23; **(10)** Luke 2:36–37; **(11)** Matthew 6:16–17; **(12)** Matthew 9:15; **(13)** Acts 13:1–3; **(14)** Acts 14:23

Resources

John Piper, *A Hunger for God*
Donald S. Whitney, *Spiritual Disciplines for the Christian Life*

21. What do we know about Jesus's second coming?

To get an overview of the sweep and context of Jesus's teaching, read Matthew 23:37–25:46.

Will Christ's second coming happen?

(1) Hebrews 9:28; **(2)** 2 Peter 3:10; **(3)** John 14:3; **(4)** Acts 1:11; **(5)** 1 Thessalonians 4:16; **(6)** James 5:8; **(7)** Revelation 1:7

Do we know *when* it will happen?

(1) Matthew 24:44; 25:13; **(2)** Mark 13:32–37; **(3)** 1 Thessalonians 5:1–4; **(4)** 2 Peter 3:1–18

How should we prepare for and anticipate it?

(1) Matthew 24:42–51; **(2)** Revelation 22:20; **(3)** Titus 2:12–13; **(4)** Philippians 3:20–21; **(5)** 1 Corinthians 16:22b; **(6)** Hebrews 10:19–39; **(7)** 1 Thessalonians 3:11–13; **(8)** 2 Thessalonians 1:5–2:5; **(9)** John 14:1–3; **(10)** Titus 2:11–14; **(11)** 2 Timothy 4:1–5; **(12)** James 5:7–8; **(13)** 1 Peter 1:13; 4:13; **(14)** 1 Corinthians 15:58

What will happen when Christ returns?

(1) Colossians 3:4; **(2)** 1 Thessalonians 4:13–18; **(3)** 1 Thessalonians 2:19–20; **(4)** 1 Thessalonians 5:23; **(5)** 2 Timothy 4:8; **(6)** 1 Corinthians 15:22–28; **(7)** Revelation 19:11–20:10; **(8)** 1 John 2:28–3:3; **(9)** Acts 3:19–21; **(10)** Philippians 3:20–21

Resources

Gregg R. Allison, *Historical Theology*, 683–701[12]
Wayne Grudem, *Systematic Theology*, 1091–139[13]
Michael Horton, *The Christian Faith*, 919–45[14]
J. I. Packer, *Concise Theology*, 250–53
Gregory Strand and William Kynes, *Evangelical Convictions*, 213–31

22. How do you describe the person and work of the Holy Spirit? How has the Spirit's ministry changed since Old Testament times?

(1) Genesis 1:2; **(2)** Numbers 11:25–30; **(3)** Ezekiel 36:25–27; **(4)** Joel 2:28–29; **(5)** Luke 3:22; 4:1, 14, 18–21; **(6)** John 3:3–8; 14:15–17; 15:26; 16:8–11, 14; **(7)** Acts 16:7; Philippians 1:19; Romans 8:9; 1 Peter 1:11; **(8)** Matthew 28:19; **(9)** Luke 12:8–12; **(10)** Acts 1:8; 2:1–4; 5:1–11; 9:31; 13:1–3; **(11)** Romans 1:4; 8:1–17, 23, 26–27; **(12)** 1 Corinthians 2:6–16; 6:19–20; 12:1–13; **(13)** 2 Corinthians 1:22; 5:5; **(14)** Galatians 5:16–26; **(15)** Ephesians 1:13–14; 2:18–22; 4:30; **(16)** 1 Thessalonians 5:19; **(17)** Titus 3:4–7; **(18)** Hebrews 10:26–31; **(19)** 2 Peter 1:19–21; **(20)** 1 John 4:13; Revelation 14:13

---

12. Allison is a historic premillennialist. In these pages he traces the development of the doctrine.

13. Grudem offers in these pages a historic premillennial interpretation.

14. In these pages Horton provides a recitation of the history of interpretation and an amillennial reading of the data, along with respectful interaction with Wayne Grudem.

If you have time, read the following texts and look for things the Spirit does or enables us to do.

> **(1)** Acts 8:29, 39; 10:19; 11:12, 28–30; 13:1–3; 15:28; 19:21; 20:22–23; Romans 8:14; 1 Corinthians 12:3; **(2)** Acts 9:31 (CSB); **(3)** Galatians 4:6; Jude 20; **(4)** 2 Corinthians 3:6; **(5)** Galatians 5:5; **(6)** Ephesians 3:4–6, 16–21; Philippians 3:3; **(7)** 1 John 4:2–6; **(8)** Acts 1:8; 4:31

In the following texts, look for things the Holy Spirit gives.

> **(1)** John 7:38–39; Romans 8:2, 6, 11, 13; **(2)** Acts 6:3, 5, 10; **(3)** Acts 7:55; **(4)** Romans 5:5; **(5)** Romans 14:17; 1 Thessalonians 1:6; **(6)** Romans 15:13; **(7)** Hebrews 2:4; **(8)** 2 Corinthians 13:14; **(9)** Micah 3:8

What are we called on *not* to do in relation to the Holy Spirit?

> **(1)** Acts 5:3–4; **(2)** Acts 5:9; **(3)** Acts 7:51; **(4)** Isaiah 63:10; **(5)** Ephesians 4:30; **(6)** 1 Thessalonians 4:8; **(7)** Hebrews 10:29; **(8)** 1 Corinthians 3:16–17

What should we do instead?

> **(1)** Luke 11:13; Acts 8:15; **(2)** Acts 5:32; **(3)** Galatians 5:16–25; **(4)** Galatians 6:8; **(5)** Ephesians 2:18; 6:18; **(6)** Ephesians 5:18–20; **(7)** Ephesians 4:1–6; **(8)** 2 Timothy 1:14

Resources

Graham A. Cole, *He Who Gives Life*
Kevin DeYoung, *The Holy Spirit*
Wayne Grudem, *Systematic Theology*, chap. 30
R. C. Sproul, *Everyone's a Theologian*, chaps. 31–36
Christopher J. H. Wright, *Knowing the Holy Spirit through the Old Testament*

23. How would you distinguish between the baptism of the Holy Spirit and the fullness of the Holy Spirit?

> **(1)** Matthew 3:11; **(2)** Luke 3:16; **(3)** Romans 8:9; **(4)** Ephesians 1:13–14; **(5)** 1 Corinthians 12:13; **(6)** 1 Corinthians 6:19; **(7)** Acts 2:4, 17–18, 33, 38; 8:15, 17–19; 10:44–47; 11:12–16; 19:1–7; **(8)** Acts 4:8, 31; 6:3, 5; 9:17; 11:24; 13:9; **(9)** Luke 1:15–17; **(10)** Ephesians 5:15–18; **(11)** Exodus 31:3; 35:31; **(12)** Micah 3:8

Other texts speak less directly to this distinction but may help round out your understanding.

(12) Numbers 11:17–29; **(13)** Judges 3:10; 6:34; 11:29; 14:6, 19; **(14)** 1 Samuel 10:6; 11:6; 16:13; **(15)** Luke 1:41, 67; **(16)** Ephesians 4:30

Resources
J. I. Packer, *Keep in Step with the Spirit*
John R. W. Stott, *Baptism and Fullness*

24. How can someone discover his or her spiritual gifts?

(1) Romans 12:4–8; **(2)** 1 Corinthians 12–14; **(3)** 1 Peter 4:10–11; **(4)** Ephesians 4:11–16

Some foundational practices include these:

1. Pray. God wants you to know your gift(s).
2. Serve. Do what you see needs doing. The fact that you see it (when others may not) may mean that God has opened your eyes to a need that he is gifting you to address. A fruitful fit or a poor fit in service can help you discern where you should serve and, by implication, what gifts you have.
3. Ask other mature Christians what they see you doing faithfully and fruitfully. Submit to leaders.
4. Use questionnaires and inventories to clarify experience, passion, and aptitude. Being talented does not necessarily mean you have a spiritual gift in that domain, but since God is the God of creation as well as redemption, he may well have given you a talent that is related to the spiritual gift he has bestowed.
5. Learn from examples.
6. Be open to ministry with or without position or title.

Resources

Bruce L. Bugbee, *What You Do Best in the Body of Christ*
Bruce L. Bugbee and Don Cousins, *Network Participant's Guide*
Sam Storms, *The Beginner's Guide to Spiritual Gifts*

25. What is the place of prayer in the economy of God?

(1) Hebrews 4:14–16; **(2)** Psalm 2:7–8; **(3)** Matthew 6:1–15; **(4)** Luke 11:1–13; **(5)** Matthew 21:18–22; **(6)** John 14:13–14; 15:7–8; 16:23–24; **(7)** James 1:5–8; 4:2–3; 5:13–18; **(8)** 1 John 3:22; **(9)** 2 Chronicles 7:14; **(10)** Proverbs 15:8, 29; 28:9; **(11)** 1 Peter 3:7; **(12)** 1 John 1:9; 5:14–15; **(13)** 1 Timothy 2:1–6; **(14)** Ephesians 2:18;[15] **(15)** Ephesians 6:18; **(16)** Acts 4:23–31; **(17)** Luke 18:1–14; **(18)** Ecclesiastes 5:1–3; Isaiah 50:4;[16] **(19)** Colossians 4:2; **(20)** 1 Peter 4:7; **(21)** Isaiah 58:9–10

Resources

D. A. Carson, *Praying with Paul*
Brian Chapell, *Praying Backwards*
Wayne Grudem, *Systematic Theology*, chap. 18
Timothy Keller, *Prayer*
Paul E. Miller, *A Praying Life*
Richard L. Pratt, *Praying with Your Eyes Open*
Philip Yancey, *Prayer*

26. How should you lead the congregation in prayer in public worship?

(1) Matthew 6:5–13;[17] **(2)** Matthew 18:19–20; **(3)** 1 Timothy 2:1–7; **(4)** Ecclesiastes 5:1–3; **(5)** 1 Corinthians 14:14–17; **(6)** James 5:16; **(7)** Colossians 4:2–4; **(8)** 1 Chronicles 29:10–20; **(9)** 1 Kings 8:22–30; **(10)** Ezra 9:4–10:1; **(11)** John 17:1–26; **(12)** Acts 4:23–30; **(13)** Philippians 1:9–11; **(14)** 1 Thessalonians 3:11–13; **(15)** Ephesians 3:14–21

15. Note how all three persons of the Trinity relate in prayer.
16. Note how listening is an important part of prayer.
17. Notice that Matthew's version tells us to pray in this manner ("Pray, then, like this"), while Luke says, "When you pray, say . . ." (11:2). The Lord's Prayer is both a pattern prayer and a set prayer.

Resources

D. A. Carson, *Praying with Paul*
Megan Hill, *Praying Together*
Samuel Miller, *Thoughts on Public Prayer*
Stuart Olyott, *Reading the Bible and Praying in Public*

27. How should you offer proactive Christian counsel?

(1) Ezekiel 34:1–19; **(2)** Jeremiah 3:15; **(3)** Matthew 9:36; **(4)** John 10:11–14; **(5)** 1 Peter 5:1–4; **(6)** Isaiah 61:1–3; **(7)** Galatians 6:1–2; **(8)** James 1:5; **(9)** Proverbs 29:20; **(10)** James 1:19–20; **(11)** Proverbs 15:23; 16:23; 25:11; **(12)** Romans 15:14; **(13)** Hebrews 3:12–14; 4:12–13; 10:19–25; **(14)** Philippians 4:5–7; **(15)** Ephesians 4:17–32; **(16)** Colossians 3:5–17; **(17)** 1 Thessalonians 5:14–15

At present, how qualified do you feel to offer this kind of counsel on the following topics?[18]

anger

fear/anxiety

depression

resentment

guilt

same-sex attraction

compulsive sins/addictions (por-
nography, gambling, alcohol,
video games, gluttony, etc.)

preparing for marriage

marital conflict

vocation

finances

bereavement/grief

parenting

crises/trauma

Resources

Andrew A. Bonar, *The Visitor's Book of Texts*
Gary R. Collins, *Christian Counseling*
David Dickson, *The Elder and His Work*
John G. Kruis, *Quick Scripture Reference for Counseling*
Timothy S. Lane and Paul David Tripp, *How People Change*
David Powlison, *Seeing with New Eyes*

18. See questions 58 and 70 for more discussion and resources related to these topics.

David Powlison, *Speaking Truth in Love*
David Short and David Searle, *Pastoral Visitation*
Paul David Tripp, *Instruments in the Redeemer's Hands*
Edward T. Welch, *Side by Side*

28. How should you comfort the bereaved?

(1) Romans 12:15; (2) James 1:19–20; (3) Galatians 6:2; (4) 2 Corinthians 1:3–4; (5) Psalms 23; 34:17–18; 73:26; 119:28; (6) Isaiah 53:3–4; (7) John 11:17–44; (8) 1 Corinthians 15:50–58; (9) 1 Thessalonians 4:13–18; (10) Hebrews 2:14–15; (11) 2 Timothy 1:10; (12) 2 Corinthians 4:14–5:8; (13) Romans 8:31–39; (14) John 14:1–6

Consider these suggestions gleaned from Nancy Guthrie's book *What Grieving People Wish You Knew about What Really Helps (and What Really Hurts)*:

1. Just go—being present is irreplaceable.
2. Listen more than you talk.
3. If you talk, share stories. Mention memories of the person who has died. Say his or her name.
4. Don't make assumptions.

Resources

Gary R. Collins, *Christian Counseling*, chap. 25
Nancy Guthrie, *What Grieving People Wish You Knew about What Really Helps (and What Really Hurts)*
D. Martyn Lloyd-Jones, *Spiritual Depression*
John Piper, *When the Darkness Will Not Lift*
Nicholas Wolterstorff, *Lament for a Son*

29. What is the human condition apart from Christ? What happens to those who have not heard the gospel when they die? What happens to those who have heard and rejected the gospel?

(1) Ephesians 2:1–3; **(2)** John 8:34; **(3)** Romans 8:5–8; **(4)** 2 Corinthians 4:4; **(5)** Romans 1:18–32; **(6)** Romans 2:12–16; 3:10–18; **(7)** John 14:6; **(8)** Acts 4:12; **(9)** Romans 10:9–18; **(10)** 1 John 5:11–12; **(11)** John 3:36; **(12)** Matthew 25:41–46; **(13)** 2 Thessalonians 1:7b–10; **(14)** Revelation 14:9–11, 17–20; 20:9–15; 21:8; **(15)** John 3:16–18

Resources
Francis Chan and Preston Sprinkle, *Erasing Hell*
Millard J. Erickson, *Christian Theology*, chap. 6
Wayne Grudem, *Systematic Theology*, chap. 56
Robert A. Peterson, *Hell on Trial*
John Piper, *Jesus*

30. What elements would you include in a three-minute version of your testimony? Write out such a version and be prepared to share it.

(1) 1 Peter 3:13–17; **(2)** Colossians 4:2–6; **(3)** Acts 17:22–31; **(4)** Ephesians 2:1–10; **(5)** Romans 3:23; 6:23; **(6)** James 2:10; **(7)** John 3:3–8, 16–18; **(8)** Romans 10:9–10; **(9)** Acts 16:31; **(10)** Acts 2:36–38; **(11)** Acts 22:1–21; 26:1–23; **(12)** 1 Corinthians 2:13; **(13)** Matthew 10:19

Consider these suggestions, several of which come from Will Metzger's book *Tell the Truth*:

- Make it personal—let it flow from your own life.
- Make it clear—don't use a lot of complex Christian jargon.
- Make it biblical—mention essential elements of the gospel.
- Make it count—people should know how to become a Christian by the time you finish.
- Make it compelling—invite a response with a closing question.

- Make it about Jesus—your story is not primarily about how your life changed but about how Jesus changes lives.

Resources

Mark Dever, *The Gospel and Personal Evangelism*
Will Metzger, *Tell the Truth*, esp. part 3 and appendix B
Rebecca Manley Pippert, *Out of the Saltshaker and into the World*
Mack J. Stiles, *Speaking of Jesus*

31. What must happen for someone to be saved? Address predestination, election, justification, repentance, rebirth, faith, and grace in your answer.

The meaning of "salvation" depends on what someone is being saved from. Many references to being saved in the Bible are used in an absolute sense; they do not specify what those who are saved are saved from. Some of the following texts specify a few of the things we are saved *from* and saved *for*. Some also address how we are saved. Some use synonyms like "deliver" or "rescue" to describe salvation.

> (1) Isaiah 45:22; (2) Luke 7:50; (3) John 10:9; (4) Acts 2:21; 4:12; (5) Acts 15:11; 16:30–31; (6) Romans 5:9–10; (7) Romans 10:1–17; (8) 1 Corinthians 1:18; (9) 2 Timothy 1:9; (10) Titus 3:5; (11) Matthew 6:13; (12) Luke 1:74; (13) 2 Corinthians 1:10; (14) Galatians 1:4; (15) 1 Thessalonians 1:10; (16) Hebrews 2:15; (17) 2 Timothy 4:18

The following texts address various things that are in some way related to the salvation of an individual. As you study them, keep in mind that the salvation of people is God's way of regaining appropriate glory for himself and reclaiming good things for his creatures.

> (1) Ephesians 1:4–5, 11; (2) Luke 9:35; Romans 16:13; 1 Peter 2:4–10; (3) Romans 1:17; 3:21–31; 5:1–21; (4) Galatians 2:16; (5) Ephesians 2:1–10; (6) James 1:18; John 3:3; (7) Luke 13:1–5; (8) Luke 24:47; (9) Acts 2:38; 3:19; 11:18; 17:30; (10) Romans 8:28–39; (11) John 1:9–17; (12) Acts 15:11; 18:27; 20:24; (13) Romans 11:5–6

Resources
Wayne Grudem, *Bible Doctrine*, 281–325[19]
Gordon R. Lewis, *Decide for Yourself*
Leon Morris, *The Apostolic Preaching of the Cross*
J. I. Packer, *Concise Theology*, 37–39, 146–68
J. I. Packer, *God's Words*, 94–168

32. What has "taking up your cross" meant to you in practice?

(1) Matthew 10:38–39; 16:24–27; **(2)** Luke 9:23–26;[20] **(3)** John 12:25–26; **(4)** Luke 14:25–33; **(5)** Philippians 2:1–11; **(6)** Philippians 3:12–21;[21] **(7)** 2 Corinthians 4:7–18

As you reflect on this question, list some of the things that it has cost you to follow Jesus and confess him before others.

(1) Romans 8:31–39; **(2)** Philippians 3:7–10; **(3)** Acts 5:41; **(4)** Colossians 1:24–29; **(5)** 1 Peter 1:6–9

Resources
Dietrich Bonhoeffer, *The Cost of Discipleship*
David Platt, *Follow Me*
John R. W. Stott, *The Cross of Christ*

33. What word pictures does the New Testament use to describe the church? What does each picture imply concerning the nature and purpose of the church?

(1) Ephesians 1:22–23; **(2)** Ephesians 2:19–22; **(3)** Hebrews 3:6; **(4)** Hebrews 12:23; **(5)** Galatians 6:10; **(6)** 1 Timothy 3:14–15; **(7)** 1 Peter 2:4–10; **(8)** 1 Corinthians 3:16–17; **(9)** John 10:14–18; **(10)** Matthew 5:13–16; **(11)** 1 Corinthians 3:6–9; **(12)** John 1:12; 1 John 3:1–2; **(13)** Philippians 3:20; **(14)** John 15:1–8; Romans 11:17–24; **(15)** Ephesians 5:22–32

19. Grudem provides an exceptionally clear and helpful ordering of the elements involved in salvation.
20. Note the additional word that Luke includes in his record of Christ's words.
21. Here Paul bears witness to his own experience.

Resources

Gregg R. Allison, *Sojourners and Strangers*
Wayne Grudem, *Systematic Theology*, chap. 44, esp. 858–59
Bruce Milne, *Know the Truth*, chap. 23
Paul Sevier Minear, *Images of the Church in the New Testament*

34. What is your attitude toward those in authority in various spheres?

(1) Matthew 28:16–20; **(2)** 1 Corinthians 15:27–28; **(3)** Ephesians 1:22–23; **(4)** Ephesians 5:24; **(5)** Hebrews 12:9; **(6)** James 4:7; **(7)** John 5:26–27; 10:18; 17:2; **(8)** Matthew 10:1; **(9)** Luke 2:41–51; **(10)** Matthew 6:10; **(11)** Matthew 26:39; **(12)** Luke 1:38; **(13)** Romans 6:13; **(14)** James 4:7; **(15)** Romans 13:1–8; Acts 5:17–32; **(16)** Acts 25:9–11; 2 Peter 2:1, 10–11; **(17)** Titus 3:1; **(18)** 1 Peter 2:13–18; 3:1; 5:5; **(19)** 1 Corinthians 16:12–16; **(20)** Ephesians 5:21–23; **(21)** Titus 2:3–5; **(22)** 2 Corinthians 10:8; 13:10; **(23)** Revelation 20:4; **(24)** Hebrews 13:17; **(25)** Numbers 27:19–20; **(26)** Deuteronomy 1:15; **(27)** Matthew 20:25–28; **(28)** Colossians 4:1; **(29)** 1 Timothy 2:1–6; **(30)** Romans 8:7; **(31)** Luke 4:6; **(32)** Luke 10:17

Resources

Jonathan Leeman, *Church Membership*, chap. 6
D. Martyn Lloyd-Jones, *Authority*
Robert Shaw, *The Reformed Faith*, 291–304

35. How are individuals initiated into the church? How does baptism relate to a person's salvation?

(1) Matthew 28:19; **(2)** Acts 2:38–41; **(3)** Acts 8:12–13, 36; 10:48; **(4)** Acts 16:13–15, 29–34; **(5)** Acts 18:8; **(6)** Acts 19:1–6; **(7)** Acts 22:16; **(8)** 1 Peter 3:18–21; **(9)** Luke 23:39–43; **(10)** Acts 8:11–13, 24;[22] **(11)** John 1:12–13; 3:14–18; **(12)** John 5:24; **(13)** John 6:47; **(14)** John 11:25–26; **(15)** John 20:30–31; **(16)** Acts 13:38–39; **(17)** Romans 1:16–17; 3:21–27; 4:5; **(18)** Galatians 3:22; **(19)** 1 Peter 1:8–9; **(20)** 1 John 5:1, 13

> Although it be a great sin to condemn or neglect this ordinance, yet grace and salvation are not so inseparably annexed unto it, as that

22. What can we determine about Simon's baptism as it relates to his salvation (or lack thereof)?

no person can be regenerated or saved without it, or that all that are baptized are undoubtedly regenerated.

—Westminster Confession, chapter 28, section 5

Reflect on some of the things that baptism signifies.

(1) Acts 22:16; (2) 1 Corinthians 6:11; (3) Galatians 3:26–29; (4) Ephesians 5:25–27; (5) Titus 3:5; (6) 1 Corinthians 12:13; (7) Romans 6:3–7

Resources
Wayne Grudem, *Bible Doctrine*, 376–86[23]
Michael Horton, *The Christian Faith*, 763–98[24]
J. I. Packer, *Concise Theology*, 212–16
Robert Shaw, *The Reformed Faith*, 338–47
Gregory Strand and William Kynes, *Evangelical Convictions*, 169–76

36. How should you disciple an individual?

(1) Luke 6:40; (2) 2 Timothy 3:10–17; (3) 1 Corinthians 11:1; (4) 1 Thessalonians 2:8; (5) 1 Timothy 4:6–5:1; (6) Matthew 28:19–20; (7) Acts 18:24–26; (8) John 8:31–32; (9) Luke 9:23–25; (10) Ephesians 4:11–18; (11) 1 Peter 4:8–11; (12) John 13:34–35; (13) Hebrews 10:24–25; (14) Galatians 6:1–2; (15) Titus 3:1–8; (16) 2 Timothy 2:2

A few brief suggestions:

Spend time: the first disciples were often with Jesus, and it showed (Acts 4:13).

Give yourself away: value others more than yourself (Phil. 2:1–11; Acts 20:24).

Seek commitment: help those you are discipling pay the price (2 Tim. 2:3–6).

23. Grudem offers a defense of the credobaptist (believer's baptism) understanding.
24. Horton provides a defense of the paedobaptist (infant baptism) understanding.

Pray: ask the Lord whom you should disciple, and prioritize prayer with and for them.

Be an example: others will follow you, so make sure your example is Christlike (1 Cor. 11:1).

Utilize the Bible and other materials: model sound interpretation; help others read widely.

Let the cream rise to the top: not all seed falls on good soil (Mark 4:14–20), but when someone proves to be fruitful, keep cultivating and watering them (1 Cor. 3:5–7).

Take them with you: more is caught than taught.

"Watch one, do one, teach one": this medical-school strategy for training surgeons is a helpful way to disciple individuals in practical skills.

Resources

Robert E. Coleman, *The Master Plan of Evangelism*
Colin Marshall and Tony Payne, *The Trellis and the Vine*
Stephen Smallman, *The Walk*

37. As you understand Scripture, who may be a member of a local church?

The New Testament does not say much about this directly. The following texts may suggest some approaches to this matter.

What do these texts add to your understanding of membership in the local church?

(1) 1 Corinthians 12:24; (2) Ephesians 2:19; 3:6; 4:25; 5:30; (3) Colossians 3:15; (4) 2 Corinthians 8:1–5[25]

25. What seems to represent God's will according to this verse?

Some texts *may* imply that the first local churches had boundaries. One could tell who was part of the church and who was not.

(1) Romans 16:5a; (2) Acts 11:22; (3) Ephesians 1:1; (4) 1 Corinthians 5:1–13; (5) 1 Corinthians 14:23; (6) Hebrews 10:23; (7) 1 Timothy 5:9

Given the limited data, many churches hold that anyone who makes a believable profession of faith is a member of the body of Christ and therefore should be eligible to join a local expression of that body. Other churches include baptized children as members in the covenant community. In practice, elders in a local church should know their own church polity and be able to explain it to parishioners who ask when or if they should join the church.

Resources

Thabiti M. Anyabwile, *What Is a Healthy Church Member?*
Mark Dever and Paul Alexander, *The Deliberate Church*
Jonathan Leeman, *Church Membership*

38. What do you do to maintain fellowship with other Christians in your own church and other churches?

To answer this question biblically, it will help to do word studies on various forms of the word "fellowship" (*koinonia*) and the word or prefix "with" (*syn*).

We have fellowship:

(1) Acts 2:42;[26] (2) Romans 11:17;[27] (3) Ephesians 2:11–22[28]

---

26. "The fellowship" = *koinonia*. The same word appears in Philippians 1:5, where it is translated "partnership" (ESV, CSB).

27. "Share" = *synkoinonos*.

28. This passage speaks of the profound unity of Jews and Gentiles using words with the *syn* prefix in verse 19 ("fellow citizens") and verse 22 ("joined together").

Notice what else we share with Christ, and therefore in a secondary sense with each other, looking for the "with" or *syn*-prefixed words in the following verses.

(1) Romans 6:8; (2) 2 Corinthians 7:3; (3) Romans 8:17; (4) Colossians 2:12–13; 3:1; (5) Ephesians 2:5–6; (6) 2 Timothy 2:11–12

We have fellowship with other Christians. Notice how people maintained or fostered it in the following texts.

(1) Romans 16:6; (2) Romans 12:13; 15:26; (3) 2 Corinthians 8:4; 9:13; (4) Hebrews 10:25; (5) 1 Corinthians 10:16; (6) 1 John 1:1–7; (7) Acts 2:44; (8) Acts 1:14; 12:12; (9) Romans 1:10; 15:30; (10) 1 Thessalonians 3:10

The New Testament phrase "one another" can also show how we foster and maintain fellowship. Here are just a few of the occurrences of that phrase.

(1) Romans 12:10, 16; 14:13; 15:5, 7, 14; 16:16; (2) 1 Corinthians 11:33; 12:25; (3) 2 Corinthians 13:11; (4) Galatians 5:13, 15, 26; (5) Ephesians 4:2, 32; 5:19, 21; (6) Colossians 3:9, 13; (7) 1 Thessalonians 4:9, 18; 5:15; (8) Hebrews 3:13; 10:24–25; (9) James 4:11 (CSB); 5:9, 16; (10) 1 Peter 1:22; 4:8–10; 5:5; (11) 1 John 1:7

Resources

Gary DeLashmutt, *Loving God's Way*
Gene Getz, *Building Up One Another*
Thomas Jones and Steve Brown, *One Another*

39. How do you maintain a good reputation with outsiders?

(1) 1 Timothy 3:7 (CSB); (2) Proverbs 22:1; (3) Ecclesiastes 7:1; (4) Proverbs 3:1–4; (5) Psalm 15; (6) Ruth 2:10–11; (7) Titus 2:1–10; (8) 1 Peter 2:12; (9) 3 John 12; (10) Acts 16:1–2; Philippians 2:19–22; (11) Acts 22:12

Resources

Timothy Keller, *Every Good Endeavor*, part 3
Derek J. Tidball, *Builders and Fools*

40. What does the New Testament teach about church leadership?

(1) Acts 14:23; 15:2; 20:17, 28; 1 Timothy 3:1–7; Titus 1:5–9;[29] **(2)** 1 Timothy 3:8–13; **(3)** Romans 16:1–2

What are the respective qualifications and duties of the leaders mentioned in the New Testament?

1. Elders

(a) 1 Timothy 3:1–7; **(b)** Titus 1:5–9; **(c)** James 5:13–15; **(d)** Acts 20:17–38; **(e)** 1 Thessalonians 5:12–13; **(f)** Philippians 1:1; **(g)** 1 Peter 5:1–5; **(h)** 1 Timothy 5:17–25; **(i)** Ephesians 4:11–13

2. Deacons

(a) Acts 6:1–7; **(b)** Philippians 1:1; **(c)** 1 Timothy 3:8–15

3. Deaconesses

(a) Romans 16:1–2; **(b)** 1 Timothy 3:11

For which roles and responsibilities are women commended? Which are apparently not affirmed or permitted?

(1) 1 Timothy 2:12; **(2)** 1 Timothy 5:9–16; **(3)** Titus 2:3–5; **(4)** 2 Timothy 1:5; 3:14; **(5)** Proverbs 31:26; **(6)** 1 Corinthians 11:5; 14:26–33; **(7)** Colossians 3:16; **(8)** Acts 18:26; **(9)** Romans 16:1–2

Resources

Thabiti M. Anyabwile, *Finding Faithful Elders and Deacons*
Benjamin L. Merkle, *40 Questions about Elders and Deacons*
Jeramie Rinne, *Church Elders*
Alexander Strauch, *Biblical Eldership*
Alexander Strauch, *The New Testament Deacon*
Cornelis Van Dam, *The Deacon*

29. Notice that three titles are used interchangeably.

41. What qualities make one an effective leader in the family?

First, note the descriptions of elders and deacons that are specifically linked to personal character and the family context.

(1) 1 Timothy 3:1–13; (2) Titus 2:1–8

Second, note additional qualities that characterize an effective leader.

(1) 1 Peter 5:5b–7; (2) 1 John 1:8–10; (3) James 1:5; 3:13–18; (4) John 13:12–17; (5) Matthew 20:25–28; (6) Ephesians 4:1–3; 6:4; (7) 1 Peter 4:8; (8) 1 John 4:7–12; (9) Ephesians 5:25–28; (10) 1 Peter 1:13–19; (11) 1 Corinthians 6:18; 10:13; (12) Hebrews 13:4; (13) 1 Timothy 4:7–8, 16; (14) Colossians 4:2; (15) 1 Timothy 2:1–8; (16) 1 Peter 3:7; (17) 1 Corinthians 9:24–27; (18) Philippians 3:12–14; (19) 2 Timothy 1:7; (20) John 14:15, 21; 15:14; (21) 2 John 1:6; (22) 2 Timothy 3:14–17; (23) Psalm 119:10–16; (24) 2 Thessalonians 3:5; (25) Hebrews 12:1–2; (26) Philippians 4:11–13; (27) 2 Thessalonians 3:6–13

Resources

Voddie Baucham Jr., *Family Shepherds*
R. Kent Hughes, *Disciplines of a Godly Man*
Dennis Rainey, *Stepping Up*
Paul David Tripp, *Parenting*
Paul David Tripp, *What Did You Expect?*
Timothy Z. Witmer, *The Shepherd Leader at Home*

42. What is the nature and function of the Lord's Supper?

(1) Exodus 12:1–28; (2) 1 Corinthians 5:7; (3) Matthew 26:26–29; (4) Mark 14:22–25; (5) Luke 22:14–23; (6) 1 Corinthians 10:14–21; (7) 1 Corinthians 11:17–34; (8) Matthew 5:23–24; (9) Revelation 19:9; (10) Acts 2:42; 20:7; (11) John 6:47–58;[30] (12) Hebrews 9:25–28; (13) John 19:30

Elders should be able to give thoughtful answers to questions such as these:

30. How do you think John 6:47–58 relates to the Lord's Supper?

107

- Who should come to the Lord's Table? When are children invited to partake?
- How does our church's view of the Lord's Supper compare with that of other Christian groups? Why do we celebrate the Lord's Supper once a month or once a week as opposed to other intervals common in other communions?
- Is the Lord's Table at our church open to Christians from other churches?
- What does it mean to drink the cup of the Lord in an unworthy manner (1 Cor. 11:27), and how does one avoid drinking the cup unworthily?
- What does it mean to "discern the body" (1 Cor. 11:29)? Does the word "body" in this context refer to Christ's body in the bread, to the reality of the unity of the church as epitomized by the label "body of Christ," or to something else?[31]
- What are some practical strategies for self-examination in preparation for the Lord's Supper?
- What benefits should one expect to experience by faith when properly receiving the Lord's Supper?

Serving elders should also reflect on how the administration of the Lord's Supper encourages the following:

- reconciliation between believers and with the Lord
- self-examination
- confession leading to appropriately "judging ourselves" (1 Cor. 11:31)
- discerning the body
- proclaiming the Lord's death in anticipation of his second coming

31. Consider how the phrase "despise the church" in 11:22 might shed light on your answer.

Resources

Gregg R. Allison, *Historical Theology*, 635–58
Wayne Grudem, *Bible Doctrine*, 386–95
Michael Horton, *The Christian Faith*, 798–823
Bobby Jamieson, *Understanding the Lord's Supper*
Thomas R. Schreiner and Matthew R. Crawford, *The Lord's Supper*
Robert Shaw, *The Reformed Faith*, 348–59
Gregory Strand and William Kynes, *Evangelical Convictions*, 176–81

43. How do you practice confession?

Keep in mind that, according to Scripture, all are called on to confess the truth about God and about ourselves.

(1) Romans 10:9; **(2)** Hebrews 3:1; 13:15; **(3)** 1 Timothy 6:12–13; **(4)** Philippians 2:11; **(5)** Proverbs 28:13; **(6)** Leviticus 26:40–42; **(7)** Psalms 32:1–5; 38:18; 51:1–19;[32] 66:18–20; **(8)** Ezra 9:4–15; **(9)** Nehemiah 1:6; **(10)** Daniel 9:1–19; **(11)** 1 John 1:5–2:2; **(12)** James 4:6–10; 5:15b–16; **(13)** 2 Samuel 12:13; **(14)** Acts 19:11–20

Resources

Dietrich Bonhoeffer, *Life Together*, chap. 5
Barbara R. Duguid and Wayne Duguid Houk, *Prone to Wander*
Wayne Grudem, *Systematic Theology*, chap. 18
John R. W. Stott, *Confess Your Sins*
Donald S. Whitney, *Praying the Bible*

44. Is it possible for someone who professes faith in Christ to lose his or her salvation? Why or why not?

It may be helpful as you study the following texts to look for warnings, promises, admonitions to persevere in faith, and for false and true bases of assurance.

(1) Hebrews 6:1–20; **(2)** Hebrews 10:19–39; **(3)** Matthew 24:9–13; **(4)** 2 Peter 2:20–21; **(5)** 1 Timothy 1:18–20; 4:1; 5:15; **(6)** 2 Timothy 2:10–13; **(7)** Matthew 7:21–23; **(8)** 1 John 2:19–20; **(9)** John 5:24; **(10)** Philippians 1:6; **(11)** John 6:38–40; 10:28–29; **(12)** Acts 13:48; **(13)** 1 John 3:9–10; 5:13; **(14)** 1 Peter 1:3–9; **(15)** 2 Timothy

---

32. Note especially verses 13–15.

2:19; **(16)** Ephesians 1:3–14; 4:30; **(17)** Romans 8:31–39; **(18)** John 17:2, 6, 9, 11, 24; **(19)** 1 Corinthians 1:8–9; **(20)** 2 Corinthians 5:17–19; **(21)** Hebrews 7:25; **(22)** 1 Thessalonians 5:23–24; **(23)** 2 Thessalonians 3:3; **(24)** 2 Timothy 1:12; 4:18; **(25)** Revelation 12:10–11; **(26)** Jude 24; **(27)** Hebrews 2:1; **(28)** Hebrews 3:6, 14; **(29)** John 8:31–32; **(30)** Colossians 1:22–23; **(31)** John 15:1–8; **(32)** Revelation 3:11; **(33)** Matthew 10:22–23; **(34)** 2 Corinthians 13:5–6; **(35)** 2 Peter 1:10–11

Resources

Gregg R. Allison, *Historical Theology*, 542–61
Wayne Grudem, *Bible Doctrine*, 336–47
Michael Horton, *The Christian Faith*, 680–86
J. I. Packer, *Concise Theology*, 241–46
Thomas R. Schreiner and Ardel B. Caneday, *The Race Set before Us*

45. How do you keep a clear conscience?

Notice situations where a clear conscience is mentioned and the extent to which conscience is a reliable guide.

(1) Romans 2:15; **(2)** Romans 13:5; **(3)** 1 Corinthians 8:7; **(4)** Hebrews 9:14; **(5)** Acts 24:16; **(6)** Romans 9:1; **(7)** 2 Corinthians 1:12; **(8)** 1 Timothy 1:5; **(9)** 1 Timothy 1:19; **(10)** 1 Peter 3:16; **(11)** 1 Corinthians 4:4; **(12)** 1 Timothy 4:2; **(13)** James 4:17

To what extent and in what ways are we to be bound by the consciences of others?

(1) 2 Corinthians 4:2; 5:11; **(2)** 2 Corinthians 8; **(3)** Romans 14:1–23

How does one deal with false guilt?

(1) 1 John 3:20; **(2)** Revelation 12:10–12

How does one deal with true guilt?

(1) 1 John 1:9; **(2)** Psalms 32:5; 51; **(3)** Proverbs 28:13–14; **(4)** Acts 8:22

Resources

J. D. Greear, *Jesus, Continued . . .*, chap. 11
R. C. Sproul, *What Can I Do with My Guilt?*

46. What is the hope of the individual believer?

(1) John 14:1–3; (2) Acts 24:15; (3) 1 Corinthians 15:1–58; (4) Luke 23:43; (5) 2 Corinthians 5:1–10; (6) Philippians 1:19–26; (7) 1 Timothy 1:1;[33] (8) Romans 15:13; (9) Romans 5:2; 8:28–30; (10) Psalm 39:7; (11) Titus 1:2; (12) 2 Thessalonians 2:16; (13) 1 Peter 1:3, 13; (14) Hebrews 3:6; 6:19; (15) Titus 2:13; (16) Colossians 1:23; (17) Psalm 23:4; (18) Romans 14:8; (19) Revelation 14:13

What can we know about death, eternal life, and heaven?

(1) Ephesians 2:1–7; (2) James 1:17–18; (3) Romans 6:13; (4) John 5:24–29; (5) 1 Thessalonians 4:13–18; (6) Romans 8:11; (7) Revelation 21:1–22:21; (8) 1 John 3:2; (9) 1 Corinthians 13:12; (10) Luke 19:11–27; (11) 1 Corinthians 3:10–15; (12) Isaiah 25:6–12

> Q. What is your only comfort, in life and in death?
>
> A. That I belong—body and soul, in life and in death—not to myself but to my faithful Savior, Jesus Christ, who at the cost of his own blood has fully paid for all my sins and has completely freed me from the dominion of the devil; that he protects me so well that without the will of my Father in heaven not a hair can fall from my head; indeed, that everything must fit his purpose for my salvation. Therefore, by his Holy Spirit, he also assures me of eternal life, and makes me wholeheartedly willing and ready from now on to live for him.
>
> —Heidelberg Catechism, question 1

Resources

Wayne Grudem, *Bible Doctrine*, 348–59
Michael Horton, *The Christian Faith*, 906–18
Mark Jones, *Faith. Hope. Love.*
J. I. Packer, *Concise Theology*, 264–67
Gregory Strand and William Kynes, *Evangelical Convictions*, 253–54

---

33. Note the description of Jesus.

47. What is your attitude toward work? What biblical texts shape that attitude?

(1) Genesis 1:26–28; 2:15; **(2)** Genesis 3:17–19; **(3)** Exodus 31:1–11; **(4)** Psalms 90:17; 127:1–2; **(5)** Proverbs 12:11, 24; 13:4; **(6)** Ecclesiastes 2:24–26; **(7)** Acts 20:32–35; **(8)** 1 Corinthians 3:5–9; 10:31; **(9)** Ephesians 4:28; 6:5–9; **(10)** Colossians 3:17; 3:22–4:1; **(11)** 1 Thessalonians 2:9–10; **(12)** 2 Thessalonians 3:6–13; **(13)** Revelation 21:22–22:5; **(14)** Matthew 25:1–30

Resources
Timothy Keller, *Every Good Endeavor*
Tom Nelson, *Work Matters*
Amy L. Sherman, *Kingdom Calling*

48. How does one pursue holiness?

(1) Leviticus 19:2; **(2)** Ephesians 1:3–4; **(3)** Hebrews 12:1–2, 14; **(4)** Psalm 119:1–3, 9–11; **(5)** Psalm 139:23–24; **(6)** Proverbs 16:17; **(7)** Romans 13:12–14; **(8)** Philippians 2:12–16a; **(9)** Philippians 4:8–9; **(10)** Romans 8:12–13; **(11)** Colossians 3:5–10; **(12)** Titus 2:11–14; **(13)** 1 Peter 1:13–16; **(14)** 1 John 1:5–10; **(15)** Hebrews 10:19–25

Resources
Jerry Bridges, *The Pursuit of Holiness*
Kevin DeYoung, *The Hole in Our Holiness*
Wayne Grudem, *Systematic Theology*, chap. 38, esp. 753–58
J. I. Packer, *Faithfulness and Holiness*

49. How do you resist sexual temptation?

(1) Genesis 39:6b–12; **(2)** Job 31:1–4; **(3)** Psalm 37:1–6; **(4)** Matthew 6:33; **(5)** Psalm 119:9–11; **(6)** Proverbs 7:6–27; **(7)** Matthew 5:27–30; **(8)** Luke 22:40; **(9)** 1 Corinthians 6:18–20; 10:8, 12–13; **(10)** Galatians 5:16–25; **(11)** Ephesians 5:1–12; **(12)** Hebrews 4:14–16; **(13)** 2 Timothy 2:22; **(14)** Titus 2:11–14; **(15)** James 5:16; **(16)** 1 John 1:5–10

Resources

Randy Alcorn, *The Purity Principle*
Joshua Harris, *Sex Is Not the Problem (Lust Is)*
Heath Lambert, *Finally Free*

50. How does legalism differ from gospel obedience?

This topic is included so you will be equipped to respond wisely when, in the course of challenging someone to disciplined obedience, they complain, "You are just being legalistic."

Daniel Doriani, in *Putting the Truth to Work* (126–28), distinguishes several types of legalism. One is "the hope of attaining or retaining salvation by works." Legalism "can also mean the act of fabricating new laws." Doriani notes that this second type can take the form of either forbidding what is permissible but not forbidden in Scripture or requiring what is merely advisable but not commanded in the Bible.

As you read the following texts, try to discern the errors they highlight and the biblical alternatives they commend.

(1) Mark 7:1–23; (2) Matthew 22:36–40; (3) Matthew 23:1–36; (4) Luke 10:25–37; (5) Matthew 5:17–20; (6) Philippians 2:12–13; (7) Ephesians 2:10; (8) Titus 2:6–8, 11–14; 3:8, 14; (9) John 15:1–17; (10) Colossians 2:16–23; (11) Deuteronomy 30:11–20; (12) 1 Corinthians 9:19–23; (13) Galatians 5:1–24; (14) Romans 5–8[34]

Resources

Dan Doriani, *Putting the Truth to Work*, 126–28
Michael Horton, *The Christian Faith*, 664–73
J. I. Packer, *Concise Theology*, 159–61, 172–77

---

34. This passage is a detailed discussion of this very important pastoral problem. Let it enrich your understanding of the liberating nature of gospel obedience.

51. How should you receive criticism?

In a fallen world, criticism is to be expected. We are not perfect; neither are our critics. Receiving criticism well is an important part of maturity in leadership. How well do you receive criticism? Think of at least one specific instance.

The following principles may help you to receive criticism appropriately.

1. Minimize reasons for criticism.
   (a) 1 Peter 3:16–17
2. Don't retaliate when criticized.
   (a) 1 Peter 2:23; (b) Romans 12:19–21
3. Rejoice in false criticism you receive because of the gospel.
   (a) Matthew 5:11–12
4. Accept and learn from valid criticism. When in doubt, assume criticism of yourself is valid.
   (a) 2 Samuel 16:5–12; (b) 2 Samuel 19:15–23; (c) 1 Kings 2:8–9, 36–46; (d) Galatians 2:11–14; (e) Acts 15:37–38; (f) 2 Timothy 4:11
5. Ask the Lord to search your heart and show you the kernel of truth in any criticism. Ask, Is this true of me? Is the criticism a moral issue requiring repentance, a judgment issue requiring growth in wisdom, or a personal preference issue requiring sensitivity? Sometimes what we feel defensive about is actually a rebuke that we need or a correction God himself wants us to make.
   (a) Psalm 139:23–24; (b) Acts 18:24–28
6. Ask the Lord for deliverance from wicked people.
   (a) Psalm 140:1–3; (b) Psalm 59:1–4
7. Defend one's office and the gospel when these are the real focus of the criticism.
   (a) 2 Corinthians 10–13

8. Forgive those who criticize you.

(a) Matthew 6:12; (b) Ephesians 4:25–32; (c) Colossians 3:13

9. Learn to criticize others effectively and appropriately, rebuking and correcting as the situation warrants and the Lord leads.

(a) 2 Timothy 4:2; (b) Proverbs 9:7–9; (c) Titus 2:15; (d) 1 Timothy 5:1

10. A growing capacity to receive criticism graciously is vital for the elder because the inability to do so may severely restrict the quantity and quality of insightful feedback others offer. Defensiveness signals to others that you may react badly to helpful but potentially painful or threatening insights they could offer. Think of the last few times you were criticized. If these are rare, it may or may not be because you are above reproach! Ask the Lord to show you in what respects you need to grow in receiving criticism.

(a) Proverbs 27:6a; (b) Colossians 3:16

Resources
John Newton, "On Controversy"
David Powlison, "Does the Shoe Fit?"

52. Who is Satan? What do we know about him from Scripture?

Understanding Satan's nature, role, and destiny is crucial for helping others resist temptation. Notice his strategies and limitations. These are foundational to grasping how we overcome his wiles.

What names or titles does the Bible use for Satan?

(1) Job 1:6; (2) Matthew 4:10; (3) Luke 10:18; (4) Matthew 4:1; 13:39; 25:41; (5) Zechariah 3:1; (6) Revelation 12:10; (7) Isaiah 14:12;[35] (8) Matthew 13:19; (9) 1 John 2:13; (10) Genesis 3:1, 14; (11) 2 Corinthians 11:3; (12) 1 John 5:18; (13) Revelation 12:9; 20:2; (14) Matthew 10:25; 12:24, 27; (15) John 12:31; 14:30; 16:11; (16) Ephesians 2:2; (17) Matthew 4:3; (18) 1 Thessalonians 3:5

35. Lucifer ("light-bearer," shining one, morning star) is a title inferred from Isaiah 14:12 KJV.

What is Satan's origin (the biblical data is limited)?

(1) Genesis 3; (2) Matthew 12:24; (3) Isaiah 14:12–15; Ezekiel 28:1–19[36]

What is Satan's character?

(1) John 8:44; (2) Revelation 12:9; (3) 2 Corinthians 4:4

What does Satan do?

(1) Genesis 3; (2) 1 Chronicles 21:1; (3) 2 Corinthians 11:3, 14; (4) Revelation 12:10; (5) Zechariah 3:1; (6) Ephesians 6:10–18; (7) 1 Corinthians 5:5; (8) Matthew 4:1–11; (9) 2 Corinthians 2:11; (10) 1 Peter 5:8

What is Satan's status?

(1) Job 1:12; 2:6; (2) Colossians 2:15; (3) 2 Peter 2:4; (4) Jude 6; (5) Ephesians 1:19–23; (6) James 4:7; (7) 1 John 4:4

What is Satan's destiny?

(1) Matthew 25:41; (2) Romans 16:20; (3) Revelation 12:7–12; 20:1–3, 7–10[37]

Resources

Gregg R. Allison, *Historical Theology*, 298–318
Thomas Brooks, *Precious Remedies against Satan's Devices*
Wayne Grudem, *Bible Doctrine*, 175–83
J. I. Packer, *Concise Theology*, 69–70

53. How do believers confront and defeat the devil?

(1) Luke 4:1–13; (2) Matthew 6:13; (3) James 4:7–8; (4) 1 Peter 5:8–9; (5) Matthew 16:18–19; (6) Luke 10:18–20; (7) Revelation 12:10–12; (8) Ephesians 4:25–27; (9) Ephesians 6:10–18; (10) 2 Timothy 2:22–25; (11) 1 John 2:13–14; (12) Romans 12:9–21; (13) Romans 8:1; (14) John 16:33; (15) 2 Thessalonians 3:3; (16) 1 John 5:18–20

36. These texts may apply in a secondary sense if these kings are "types" of Satan.
37. The whole book of Revelation chronicles, among other things, what will happen to Satan and his fellow fallen angels. These passages are the most explicit.

Resources

Neil Anderson, *The Bondage Breaker*
Brian Borgman and Rob Ventura, *Spiritual Warfare*
Wayne Grudem, *Systematic Theology*, chap. 20

54. What is your plan to maintain physical fitness?

What attitudes should we have toward our bodies?

(1) 1 Corinthians 6:19–20; **(2)** 1 Corinthians 9:24–27

What dangers should we be alert to?

(1) Romans 1:24; **(2)** Philippians 3:17–19; **(3)** Proverbs 25:16; **(4)** Proverbs 22:13; 26:14

To what extent should you prioritize physical training?

(1) 1 Timothy 4:6–10;[38] **(2)** 2 Timothy 2:1–7;[39] **(3)** Mark 6:31;[40] **(4)** Psalm 55:6–8[41]

List the bodily disciplines you regularly pursue, and prepare to talk with your fellow trainees concerning changes you might profitably make.

Resources

Kori Carter, *The Christian Athlete Training Journal*
Darrin Patrick and Amie Patrick, *The Dude's Guide to Marriage*, chaps. 4 and 9
John Piper, *Brothers, We Are Not Professionals*, chap. 27

---

38. It is a judgment call whether the best rendering of verse 8 is "Bodily training profits little" or "Bodily training profits a little."
39. What do the soldier, athlete, and farmer have in common?
40. Think of the importance of rest.
41. What is the value of getting away?

55. What constitutes heresy? How should church leaders respond to it?

As you read these texts, try to distinguish various levels of error and corresponding responses.

(1) Jeremiah 23:32; (2) Matthew 22:29–33; 24:4–5, 11; (3) John 8:32–47; (4) Acts 15:1–41; (5) Romans 14:1–23; (6) 1 Corinthians 1:10–17; 3:1–23; 11:18–19; (7) 1 Corinthians 6:1–11; (8) 1 Corinthians 8:1–13; (9) 1 Corinthians 15; (10) 2 Corinthians 13:1–10; (11) Galatians 1:6–10;[42] (12) Philippians 4:2–3; (13) 2 Thessalonians 2:3; 3:6–12; (14) 1 Timothy 1:3–11, 18–20; 4:1–5; (15) Titus 1:10–16; 3:9–11; (16) 2 Peter 1:16–2:3; (17) 1 John 2:21–27; 3:4–10; 4:1–6; (18) Colossians 2:6–23

Resources
Harold O. J. Brown, *Heresies*
Justin S. Holcomb, *Know the Creeds and Councils*
Justin S. Holcomb, *Know the Heretics*

56. What sorts of conflict should you be prepared to encounter in the church? How does a godly leader address conflict?

First, consider the kinds of conflict you might encounter as a church leader.

(1) Galatians 2:11–14; (2) Acts 15:36–41; (3) Numbers 12:1–3; (4) Matthew 12:46–50; (5) 1 Corinthians 6:1; (6) Philippians 3:2–3; (7) Philemon 8–22; (8) Acts 4:1–3; 19:23–34; (9) Acts 6:1–7; (10) Acts 17:5–8; (11) 2 Timothy 4:9–10, 14–15; (12) Acts 15:1–5; (13) Colossians 2:8–23; (14) 2 Timothy 3:1–9; (15) 2 Peter 2:1–3

In addition, consider these potential conflicts:

- Marital conflicts
- Parent/child conflicts
- Generational conflicts
- Conflicts between staff members

42. The whole letter supplies the necessary context.

- Conflicts between a church and supported missionaries
- Conflicts over money
- Conflicts over leadership decisions, style, vision
- Conflict with another church or with a denomination

Second, consider what principles might undergird your approach to conflict as an elder of God's people.

(1) Romans 3:23; (2) 1 John 1:8–10; (3) 1 Timothy 1:15; (4) Proverbs 10:12; 15:18; 16:28; 28:25; 29:2; (5) James 4:1–3; (6) Proverbs 15:1; (7) Matthew 5:38–42; (8) Ephesians 4:25–32; (9) 1 Peter 3:8–12; (10) Ephesians 4:1–3; (11) Philemon 1–4; (12) James 1:19–20; (13) Romans 12:17–21; (14) 1 Timothy 2:1–4; (15) Luke 17:3; (16) Matthew 18:15–17; (17) Revelation 2:21a; (18) 1 Timothy 1:3–4; 4:1–6; 6:3–5, 17–19; (19) 2 Timothy 4:1–4; (20) Titus 1:9–14; 3:10–11; (21) 1 Timothy 4:7; (22) 2 Timothy 2:14–18, 23–26; (23) Titus 3:9; (24) Romans 13:1–7; (25) Titus 3:1–2; (26) Acts 4:5–20; (27) Matthew 5:25–26

Resources

Timothy S. Lane and Paul David Tripp, *Relationships*
Ken Sande, *The Peacemaker*
Ken Sande and Kevin Johnson, *Resolving Everyday Conflict*
Alexander Strauch, *If You Bite and Devour One Another*

57. What sorts of strategies should we use to maintain the priority of corporate, public worship?

What lessons might validly be drawn from practices recorded in the Old Testament?

(1) 1 Chronicles 6:31–48; 15:19–22; 16:41–42; 23:5; 25:1–3; (2) Psalms 92:1–3; 95:1–11; 150:1–6; (3) 1 Kings 8:1–66; (4) 2 Samuel 6:1–23; (5) 1 Chronicles 13:8; 15:16, 28; (6) 1 Chronicles 24–25; (7) Psalm 100:1–5; (8) Psalm 22:27

What does the New Testament teach about corporate worship?

(1) Matthew 4:8–10; (2) Romans 12:1–2; (3) John 2:19–22; 4:20–24; 20:28–29; (4) Acts 2:42–47; (5) Revelation 4:10; 5:14; 7:11; 11:16; 19:4; (6) Luke 2:43; 4:16; 22:39;

(7) Acts 17:2; **(8)** Acts 20:7; **(9)** 1 Corinthians 16:2; **(10)** 1 Peter 2:4–5; **(11)** Hebrews 10:24–25; **(12)** Philippians 2:9–10; **(13)** Revelation 5:6–14; 7:9–12

Resources

Bryan Chapell, *Christ-Centered Worship*
Mike Cosper, *Rhythms of Grace*
Bob Kauflin, *Worship Matters*
Leland Ryken, James C. Wilhoit, and Tremper Longman III, eds., *Dictionary of Biblical Imagery*, 969–73

58. How do you discern the will of God—for your life, for the church, for the world?

First, summarize explicit articulations of God's will in Scripture.

(1) 1 Thessalonians 4:1–8; **(2)** Romans 8:29; **(3)** Ephesians 1:9–10; **(4)** 1 Peter 2:11–17; **(5)** Hosea 6:6; **(6)** John 6:35–40; **(7)** Deuteronomy 29:29

Second, identify factors that will help you discern God's will when it is not explicit.

(1) Ephesians 4:27; 6:11; **(2)** 1 Timothy 3:6–7; **(3)** James 4:7; **(4)** 1 Peter 5:8; **(5)** Romans 12:1–3; **(6)** 2 Corinthians 3:18; **(7)** Psalm 25:4–5; **(8)** Colossians 1:9–12; **(9)** Hebrews 13:20–21; **(10)** Matthew 9:35–38; **(11)** Ephesians 3:16–19; **(12)** Philippians 1:9–11; **(13)** James 1:5; **(14)** 2 Thessalonians 1:11–12; **(15)** Ephesians 5:15–21; **(16)** Romans 12:6–8; **(17)** Proverbs 12:15; 15:22; 19:20; **(18)** Psalm 32:8–9; **(19)** Acts 16:6–10; **(20)** Romans 15:20; **(21)** 1 Corinthians 16:8–9; **(22)** Ezra 1:1, 5; 7:27; **(23)** Nehemiah 2:12; 7:5; **(24)** 2 Corinthians 8:16

Resources

Kevin DeYoung, *Just Do Something*
Phillip D. Jensen and Tony Payne, *Guidance and the Voice of God*
John MacArthur, *Found*
R. C. Sproul, *Can I Know God's Will?*
Bruce Waltke, *Finding the Will of God*

59. What is the role of grace in the life of a believer?

First, identify the source of grace.

(1) Exodus 34:6–7; (2) John 1:14, 16–17; (3) 2 Peter 1:2

Second, identify the role grace plays in salvation.

(1) Romans 3:20–26; (2) Ephesians 2:5–10; (3) Colossians 2:13–14; (4) 2 Timothy 1:9

Third, identify the ongoing role grace plays in sanctifying our lives, motivating our actions, and shaping our relationships.

(1) Psalm 103:8–12; (2) Matthew 5:7; 6:14–15; 18:21–35; (3) Romans 1:1–5; (4) Ephesians 3:7–8; (5) Romans 5:2; (6) Romans 6:1–23; (7) 1 Corinthians 15:1–10; (8) 2 Corinthians 8:1–9; (9) 2 Corinthians 12:8–10; (10) Ephesians 4:7–13; (11) 1 Peter 4:10; (12) Colossians 4:6; (13) 2 Thessalonians 2:16–17; (14) 2 Timothy 2:1; (15) Hebrews 13:9; (16) Titus 2:11–12; (17) Hebrews 4:16; (18) Hebrews 12:14–15; (19) James 4:6

Resources

Jerry Bridges, *The Discipline of Grace*
Jerry Bridges, *The Gospel for Real Life*
Jerry Bridges, *Transforming Grace*
Bryan Chapell, *Holiness by Grace*
Gloria C. Furman, *Glimpses of Grace*
J. I. Packer, *God's Words*, 94–108

60. What should be a Christian's attitude and practice with regard to giving money?

(1) Proverbs 3:9–10; (2) Exodus 34:26a; 35:4–29; (3) Haggai 1:1–11; (4) Malachi 3:6–12; (5) 1 Corinthians 16:2; (6) 2 Corinthians 8:1–9:15; (7) Galatians 6:6–9; (8) Philippians 4:10–20; (9) 1 John 3:16–18; (10) Romans 12:3–13; (11) Romans 15:23–33; (12) Matthew 6:1–4, 19–24; (13) 1 Timothy 6:3–19

Resources

Randy Alcorn, *Managing God's Money*
Randy Alcorn, *The Treasure Principle*
John R. W. Stott, *The Grace of Giving*

61. How do you preserve your integrity?

First, describe the value of integrity.

(1) Proverbs 11:3; **(2)** Proverbs 12:22; 21:3; 28:6; **(3)** Proverbs 20:7; **(4)** Psalm 41:11–12; **(5)** Daniel 6:1–5

Second, describe how you preserve your integrity.

(1) Colossians 1:21–23a; **(2)** Psalms 1:1–6; 119:1–16; **(3)** Philippians 2:12–16; **(4)** Acts 24:16; 1 Peter 3:13–17; **(5)** Ephesians 4:20–5:1; **(6)** Psalm 32:3–5; **(7)** James 5:15–16; **(8)** 2 Corinthians 7:1–2; 8:21; **(9)** Matthew 5:48; **(10)** Luke 6:27–36; **(11)** Romans 12:9–10; **(12)** Acts 23:1; 24:16; **(13)** 2 Corinthians 4:2; **(14)** Psalm 139:23–24; **(15)** Hebrews 13:18; **(16)** Romans 12:2; **(17)** Philippians 4:8–9; **(18)** Proverbs 4:20–27; **(19)** 1 Timothy 4:16; **(20)** Proverbs 21:23; **(21)** James 1:19–26; **(22)** Proverbs 2:1–22; **(23)** 1 Timothy 6:6–10; **(24)** Luke 17:3; **(25)** Hebrews 10:23–25

Resources

Jerry Bridges, *The Practice of Godliness*
Dan Doriani, *The New Man*
R. Kent Hughes, *Disciplines of a Godly Man*, chap. 10
John MacArthur, *The Power of Integrity*

62. How do you keep yourself free from the love of money?

(1) 1 Timothy 6:6–11; **(2)** Hebrews 13:5–7; **(3)** Matthew 6:19–33; **(4)** Romans 8:1–17; **(5)** Galatians 5:16–25; **(6)** Romans 12:1–13; **(7)** Philippians 4:11–13; **(8)** 1 John 2:15–17; **(9)** 1 Peter 4:7–11; **(10)** John 14:1–3

Resources

Randy Alcorn, *Money, Possessions, and Eternity*
Timothy Keller, *Counterfeit Gods*
Paul David Tripp, *Sex and Money*

63. How do you pursue humility?

(1) Titus 3:3–7; **(2)** Ephesians 2:1–10; **(3)** Matthew 23:12; **(4)** Romans 12:3; **(5)** Ephesians 4:1–3; **(6)** Colossians 3:12–13; **(7)** James 4:10; **(8)** Jeremiah 10:6; **(9)** Psalm 96:4–6; **(10)** Romans 11:33–36; **(11)** Psalm 8:1–4; **(12)** Hebrews 12:1–2; **(13)** Psalm 25:8–9; **(14)** Proverbs 22:4; **(15)** Philippians 2:5–11; **(16)** Matthew 11:28–30; 20:25–28; **(17)** Luke 18:9–14; **(18)** Romans 3:23; **(19)** Luke 14:7–11; **(20)** Philippians 2:1–4; **(21)** Ecclesiastes 5:2; **(22)** James 1:19; **(23)** Proverbs 11:2; **(24)** Romans 12:16; **(25)** 1 Peter 5:5–7; **(26)** Romans 12:3–10; **(27)** John 13:12–15; **(28)** Galatians 5:13; **(29)** 1 Thessalonians 5:25; **(30)** James 5:16; **(31)** Proverbs 27:17; **(32)** Luke 17:3; **(33)** Galatians 6:1–2; **(34)** John 15:1–6; **(35)** 1 Corinthians 4:6–7; **(36)** 1 Peter 4:11

Resources

Jerry Bridges, *The Blessing of Humility*
John Dickson, *Humilitas*
Andrew Murray, *Humility*

64. What does it mean to "live with your [wife] in an understanding way" (1 Pet. 3:7)?

(1) 1 Peter 3:1–7;[43] **(2)** Ephesians 5:15–33; **(3)** Colossians 3:19; **(4)** Proverbs 31:10–31; **(5)** Proverbs 11:16a; **(6)** Song of Solomon[44]

43. The CSB translates verse 7 as "Husbands, in the same way, live with your wives in an understanding way, as with a weaker partner, showing them honor as coheirs of the grace of life, so that your prayers will not be hindered." Young's Literal Translation renders it "The husbands, in like manner, dwelling with [them], according to knowledge, as to a weaker vessel—to the wife—imparting honour, as also being heirs together of the grace of life, that your prayers be not hindered." As you give prayerful thought to this verse in its context, it may help to ask the Lord to guide you in discerning your wife's weaknesses so that you can offer support and encouragement. How can you grow in understanding of her? What are you doing consistently to know her better? How do you honor her in ways appropriate to her strengths and weaknesses? Meditate on how God's grace underscores your profound equality. Don't miss the truth that prayer and a good relationship with your wife are not unrelated.

44. Song of Solomon provides abundant language for affirmation of physical beauty!

Resources
Dan Doriani, *The New Man*
Timothy Keller, *The Meaning of Marriage*

65. What are your personal habits with regard to planning? What biblical principles undergird and shape planning?[45]

(1) Proverbs 3:5–6, 29; **(2)** Proverbs 16:1, 3, 9; 20:18; **(3)** Isaiah 30:1–2; **(4)** Acts 2:22–24; **(5)** Ephesians 1:3–10; 3:9; **(6)** Acts 5:38; **(7)** James 4:13–17; **(8)** Psalm 37; **(9)** 1 Chronicles 28:1–21; **(10)** 2 Corinthians 1:15–2:17; **(11)** Acts 9:6, 15–16; 20:22–24

Resources
David Allen, *Getting Things Done*
Tim Challies, *Do More Better*
Matt Perman, *What's Best Next*

66. How can one impart vision?

"Vision" in the Bible almost never means what leaders have in mind when they speak of "casting vision." Such leaders tend to refer to vision as the preferred future of the church. Unfortunately, the source of that vision may be questionable. Our intention, in contrast with relying on faulty sources of vision, is to let Scripture inform leaders of God's preferred ideal of the church. With this clearly in mind, leaders can then seek to discern corporately which part of the task of conforming to that ideal needs to be emphasized now. Here is a sample of biblical instances of vision.

(1) Genesis 15:1; **(2)** Numbers 12:6; **(3)** 1 Samuel 3:1; **(4)** 2 Chronicles 32:32; **(5)** Jeremiah 14:14; **(6)** Ezekiel 7:26; **(7)** Ezekiel 11:24; **(8)** Ezekiel 12:27; **(9)** Daniel 8:17, 26–27; **(10)** Micah 3:4–8; **(11)** Habakkuk 2:2–3; **(12)** Matthew 17:1–9; **(13)** Acts 9:10–15; **(14)** Acts 10:3, 9–23; **(15)** Acts 16:9–10; **(16)** Acts 18:9; **(17)** Acts 26:19

---

45. Questions 65–68 have in view certain leadership skills needed to give direction to a church. Our primary goal is that you grow in these areas so that you will be a more effective elder. It is possible you may also, one day, be called to help congregation members grow along these lines.

Proverbs 29:18 is sometimes quoted as if it calls for what contemporary organizational leaders seek to promote, perhaps based on the KJV: "Where there is no vision, the people perish: but he that keepeth the law, happy is he." More accurate is the CSB: "Without revelation people run wild, but one who follows divine instruction will be happy." The ESV renders it "Where there is no prophetic vision the people cast off restraint, but blessed is he who keeps the law." The idea is that without a word from the living God people have no ethical or spiritual direction; with it, when they obey it, they are blessed.

Is there then biblical warrant for setting before God's people a vivid mental image of what God desires for his people, individually and corporately? A case can be made that the New Testament Epistles, by offering correctives and commands for churches and their leaders, are creating a picture of what the church should be. Paul does this with particular power in several of his letters.

(1) Ephesians 1:15–23; **(2)** Philippians 1:9–11; **(3)** Colossians 1:9–14; **(4)** 1 Thessalonians 1:2–10; **(5)** 2 Thessalonians 1:11–12

A word of caution: telling fellow believers what you are praying for them and the church is a powerful communication tool; don't wield it unless you are actually praying for these things.

God's vision for his preferred future of his people is not bounded by this age. Make sure your vision casting includes God's ultimate vision for all things.

(1) Romans 8:18–25; **(2)** 2 Corinthians 4:16–18; **(3)** 1 Peter 5:10–11; **(4)** Revelation 21:1–4

Resources

Dan Allender, *Leading with a Limp*
Leighton Ford, *Transforming Leadership*
R. Albert Mohler Jr., *The Conviction to Lead*
John Piper, *The Marks of a Spiritual Leader*
J. Oswald Sanders, *Spiritual Leadership*

67. How do you steward your time—your daily calendar, tasks, rhythms, and year?

(1) Ephesians 5:15–17; (2) Colossians 4:5; (3) John 9:4; (4) Psalm 90:9–12; (5) Esther 4:14; (6) Romans 13:11–14; (7) 2 Peter 3:8–14; (8) James 4:13–17; (9) Psalm 39:4–5; (10) Proverbs 16:9; (11) Ecclesiastes 3:1–14; (12) Mark 1:15; (13) 2 Corinthians 5:20–6:2; (14) Hebrews 3:12–15; (15) 2 Timothy 4:1–2; (16) Proverbs 24:27; (17) Nehemiah 2:11–15; (18) Luke 14:28–30; (19) Psalms 5:3; 27:14; 123:2; (20) Hosea 12:6; (21) Luke 10:38–42; (22) Matthew 6:31–34; (23) Isaiah 32:8; (24) Proverbs 16:3; 20:18; (25) Mark 1:35–38[46]

Resources

Kevin DeYoung, *Crazy Busy*

Jonathan Edwards, "The Resolutions of Jonathan Edwards"

68. What should you keep in mind when leading any kind of church meeting, whether a meeting of a board, committee, task force, or the whole congregation?

The New Testament records the details of only a few church meetings. What do you glean from these records?

(1) Acts 2:42–47; (2) Acts 13:1–3; (3) Acts 15:1–41

The best answers to this question are in the realm of wisdom that is applicable in any setting, including church meetings of assorted sizes. The following proverbs are a sample of the scriptural wisdom that relates especially to meetings. Many texts speak of things that should be in place *before* a meeting occurs. Many also speak of the kinds of coworkers you should ask the Lord to supply, and the kinds who you fervently hope will not be entrusted with leadership in the church.

(1) Proverbs 1:7; (2) Proverbs 2:1–15; (3) Proverbs 4:23–27; (4) Proverbs 11:12–14, 28; (5) Proverbs 12:15–16; 13:10, 18, 20; (6) Proverbs 14:4, 15–16, 29; (7) Proverbs 15:1; (8) Proverbs 16:1, 3, 9, 18–21; (9) Proverbs 17:9, 14, 27–28; (10) Proverbs 18:17;

46. Know your purpose, God's calling for you.

(11) Proverbs 19:11; **(12)** Proverbs 20:5, 22; **(13)** Proverbs 21:5; **(14)** Proverbs 22:23–24, 30–31; **(15)** Proverbs 22:1–4, 24–27; **(16)** Proverbs 24:1–4, 10–11, 13–20, 27–29; **(17)** Proverbs 25:12, 15, 19; **(18)** Proverbs 26:12, 17, 21; **(19)** Proverbs 27:1–2, 6, 21; **(20)** Proverbs 28:18, 23, 26; **(21)** Proverbs 29:11, 20, 22–23, 25; **(22)** Proverbs 30:32

Resources

Dick Axelrod and Emily Axelrod, *Let's Stop Meeting Like This*
Patrick Lencioni, *Death by Meeting*
Alexander Strauch, *Meetings That Work*

69. What do you do to control your tongue?

First, notice the potential danger of the tongue.

(1) Psalm 52:1–5; **(2)** Proverbs 5:3–5; 7:21; **(3)** Proverbs 6:2–3; **(4)** Proverbs 10:8; 18:7; **(5)** Proverbs 10:19; **(6)** Proverbs 11:9; **(7)** Proverbs 16:27; **(8)** Proverbs 18:6; **(9)** Proverbs 18:13; **(10)** Proverbs 18:21; **(11)** Proverbs 26:20–28; **(12)** James 3:1–12

Second, notice the potential blessing of the tongue.

(1) Proverbs 8:6–11; **(2)** Proverbs 11:13; **(3)** Proverbs 15:1–2; **(4)** Proverbs 15:23, 28; **(5)** Proverbs 16:21; **(6)** Proverbs 21:23; **(7)** Proverbs 25:11–12, 15

Third, glean general wisdom about the use of the tongue.

(1) Ecclesiastes 5:1–7; **(2)** Deuteronomy 23:21–23; **(3)** Mark 7:6–13; **(4)** James 5:12; **(5)** Psalm 141:3; **(6)** Matthew 12:33–37; 15:10–20; **(7)** Proverbs 4:24; **(8)** Ephesians 4:25–5:4; **(9)** Colossians 4:6; **(10)** Titus 3:1–2; **(11)** James 1:19–26; **(12)** James 2:12–13; **(13)** James 4:11–12; **(14)** 1 Peter 3:10–12; **(15)** 1 Peter 4:10–11

Resources

R. Kent Hughes, *Disciplines of a Godly Man*, chap. 11
John Piper and Justin Taylor, eds., *The Power of Words and the Wonder of God*
Paul David Tripp, *War of Words*

70. How do you deal with emotional or behavioral issues as you pursue transparent godliness?

First, consider the following general pattern of transformation for believers.[47] (This pattern can be applied to a specific issue, whether a negative emotion, sin, destructive habit, temptation, or failing.)

1. *Christ's lordship.* Consider the lordship of Christ, his righteousness, sovereignty, holiness, authority; consider the claim he lays on your life; consider his character particularly in relation to the issue you have in mind.

   (a) Matthew 28:18–20; (b) Luke 6:46; (c) John 14:15, 21; (d) Acts 2:36; (e) Philippians 2:8–11; (f) Romans 10:9

2. *Your sinfulness.* Consider how far short you fall of Christ's righteousness in your own strength and how you reject his authority, desires, and standards, particularly in relation to the specific issue you are considering.

   (a) Romans 3:23; (b) Galatians 5:13–25; (c) James 2:10; (d) 1 John 1:8, 10

3. *Jesus's capacity to save.* Consider how Christ's ability to save matches your great need for Christ's forgiveness, power, and resources, particularly in relation to your specific issue.

   (a) Luke 2:10–11; 19:10; (b) Acts 4:12; (c) Romans 1:16–17; (d) 1 Corinthians 10:13; (e) Ephesians 1:3–14, 18–20; 3:20; (f) Philippians 3:20; (g) Colossians 3:1–17; (h) 1 Timothy 1:15; (i) 2 Timothy 1:9–10; (j) Titus 3:3–7; (k) Hebrews 4:14–16; 7:25; 12:1–17

4. *The necessity of faith.* Rely on the finished work of Christ on the cross and on his unfinished work interceding for you in heaven. Rely also on the power and resources available to you in Christ

---

47. This pattern for transformation is adapted from the teaching of Scott Lothery, executive pastor of the Orchard Evangelical Free Church, Arlington Heights, IL.

and by the promised Holy Spirit. Put your faith in Christ, and do so particularly in relation to specific issues.

This means (a) believing that Christ has won the victory and given you in him power to fight the specific issue, (b) actually fighting the specific issue by pursuing obedience and mortifying the flesh, (c) trusting the promises of Christ with regard to the specific issue, and (d) meditating on Scripture so that your thoughts, emotions, actions, and decisions are transformed with regard to the specific issue.

Second, work through this general pattern of transformation with regard to any specific issues you face. The list of issues and related Scriptures below may help.[48]

Boredom, indifference, complacency, or apathy

(1) Proverbs 24:33–34; (2) Zephaniah 1:12–13; (3) Mark 10:43b–45; (4) John 2:13–17; (5) Romans 12:11; (6) Galatians 6:9; (7) Ephesians 5:15–16; (8) Philippians 1:21; (9) Colossians 3:1–4; (10) 1 Thessalonians 5:2–6; (11) Revelation 3:1b–2

Discouragement or disappointment

(1) Joshua 1:9; (2) 2 Chronicles 15:7; (3) Psalms 30:4–5; 34:17–18; 37:23–24; 42:1–43:5; 73:1–28; (4) Proverbs 23:17–18; (5) Isaiah 41:10; (6) Jeremiah 29:11–14; (7) Lamentations 3:22–23; (8) Jonah 4:2; (9) Mark 10:27; (10) Romans 8:28–29; (11) Galatians 6:9; (12) Philippians 4:6–7, 13; (13) Colossians 3:23–24; (14) Titus 2:13–14; (15) Hebrews 12:1–3; (16) 1 Peter 5:10–11; (17) 2 Peter 3:8–9

Doubt

(1) Genesis 18:10–14; (2) Proverbs 3:5–8; (3) Jeremiah 32:27; (4) Matthew 11:1–11; 14:31; 21:21; 28:16–20; (5) Mark 9:24; (6) Luke 1:18–20; 24:36–49; (7) John 20:24–29; (8) Acts 14:15–17;[49] 17:30–31; (9) 1 Corinthians 15:3–8; (10) Hebrews 11:1, 6; (11) James 1:5–8; (12) 1 John 5:14–15; (13) Jude 22

---

48. The verses offered in this section can be used as part of step 4.d outlined above.

49. Notice the "witness" that God left to point to his existence and gracious providence.

Embarrassment, shame, or people pleasing

(1) Proverbs 6:1–5; 29:25; (2) Isaiah 61:7; (3) Mark 2:15–17; 6:25–26; (4) John 12:42–43; (5) Acts 4:29; 5:28–29; 10:27–29; (6) Romans 5:4–5; 9:33; (7) 2 Corinthians 5:9; (8) Galatians 1:10; (9) Ephesians 6:7; (10) Colossians 3:23–24; (11) 1 Thessalonians 2:3–6; (12) 1 Peter 2:6; 3:15–17; (13) 1 John 2:28

Envy or jealousy

(1) Exodus 20:17; (2) Deuteronomy 6:13–15; (3) Psalm 73; (4) Psalm 37:1–7; (5) Proverbs 5:15–17; 14:30; 27:4; (6) Song of Solomon 8:6; (7) Isaiah 42:8; (8) 1 Corinthians 3:2b–4; 13:4–7; (9) 2 Corinthians 12:9–10; (10) Philippians 4:11–13; (11) 1 Timothy 6:6–12; (12) James 3:13–18; 4:1–2; (13) 1 John 2:15–16

Frustration or impatience

(1) Exodus 32:1; (2) Numbers 20:1–13; (3) Psalms 27:14; 37:7; (4) Lamentations 3:24–26; (5) Jonah 4:1–11; (6) Matthew 11:28–30; (7) John 16:33; (8) 1 Corinthians 4:5; 15:58; (9) 2 Corinthians 4:16–18; (10) Galatians 4:9–11;[50] 6:9; (11) Philippians 1:6; (12) Colossians 3:23–24; (13) 1 Peter 5:7; (14) 2 Peter 3:8–9

Guilt

(1) Psalm 103:11–12; (2) Isaiah 1:18; (3) John 3:17–18; (4) Romans 3:23–24; 5:1–2; 6:23; 8:1, 33–34; (5) 2 Corinthians 5:21; (6) Ephesians 1:7; 2:8–9; (7) Hebrews 9:14; 10:19–22; (8) 1 John 1:9

Hurt, wounds, or betrayal

(1) Deuteronomy 32:39; (2) Job 5:17–18; 19:13–19; (3) Psalms 27:1–10; 41:1–13; 55:1–23; 124:1–8; 141:3–5; (4) Proverbs 27:6; (5) Ecclesiastes 7:21–22; (6) Isaiah 53:4–6; (7) Hosea 6:1–3; (8) Matthew 5:10–12; 6:14–15; 18:21–35; 26:47–56; (9) Mark 11:25; (10) Luke 22:56–61; 23:34; (11) Romans 8:31–34; 12:14–19; (12) 2 Corinthians 1:3–5; (13) 2 Timothy 4:10, 16–18; (14) Hebrews 12:3; (15) 1 Peter 2:23

---

50. Notice that Paul's frustration with the Galatians flows from his loyalty to the gospel.

Irritation, anger, or rage

(1) Exodus 34:6–7; (2) Psalms 4:4–5; 37:8–9; (3) Proverbs 12:16; 14:17, 29; 15:1, 15, 18; 19:19; 29:22; (4) Ecclesiastes 7:9; (5) Matthew 5:21–22; 18:21–22; (6) Romans 1:18; 12:18; (7) 2 Corinthians 7:8–11;[51] (8) Ephesians 4:26–27, 31; (9) Colossians 3:8, 12–15; (10) James 1:19–20; (11) 1 Peter 1:22; 3:8–9

Pride, superiority, or contempt

(1) Deuteronomy 8:17–18a; (2) Proverbs 8:13; 11:2; 16:5, 18; 26:12; 27:2; 29:23; (3) Jeremiah 9:23–24; (4) Obadiah 1:3–4; (5) Luke 15; 18:9–14; (6) Romans 11:17–21; 12:3, 16–18; (7) 1 Corinthians 4:7; 5:6–8; (8) 2 Corinthians 10:12–18; (9) Galatians 6:2–5; (10) Philippians 2:3–4; (11) 2 Timothy 3:1–5; (12) James 4:6–10; (13) 1 Peter 5:5–7; (14) Revelation 3:17–20

Resentment or bitterness

(1) Genesis 37:3–4; 50:18–21; (2) Job 21:25; (3) Isaiah 38:15–17; (4) Jonah 4:1–11; (5) Matthew 20:20–28; (6) Mark 11:25; (7) Acts 8:20–24; (8) Romans 3:9–18; 12:9–21; (9) 1 Corinthians 13; (10) Luke 12:15; (11) Ephesians 4:1–3, 31–32; (12) Colossians 3:13; (13) Hebrews 12:14–15; (14) James 3:13–18; (15) 1 John 4:7–11

Sadness or despair

(1) 2 Samuel 18; (2) 1 Kings 19:1–8; (3) Job 16:6–17:1; (4) Psalms 6; 27:13; 31:11–12; 34:17–20; (5) Isaiah 53:4; (6) Jeremiah 31:7–14; (7) Lamentations 1:1–2, 16, 21–22; 2:11–12, 18; (8) Matthew 26:36–42; (9) Luke 4:16–21; 27:27–31; (10) Romans 5:3–5; 15:13; (11) 2 Corinthians 4:8–10; (12) John 11:17–44; (13) Philippians 4:6–7; (14) Hebrews 4:15–16; (15) Revelation 21:3–4

Stress

(1) Psalms 23:1–3; 55:22; 59:16–17; 94:17–19; 118:5–6; 127:1–2; (2) Proverbs 16:3; (3) Isaiah 26:3; 40:31; (4) Jeremiah 31:25; (5) Matthew 11:28–30; (6) Mark 6:30–31; (7) Luke 6:48; 10:41–42; 21:19; (8) John 14:27; 15:4–5; (9) Acts 3:19–21; (10) 2 Corinthians 4:7–9; 12:9; (11) Philippians 4:6–7, 13; (12) James 1:2–4

---

51. Notice that "indignation" in v. 11 is positive.

Worry, anxiety, or fear

(1) Joshua 1:6–9; (2) Psalms 23:4; 55:22; 56:3; 61:1–2; 94:19; (3) Proverbs 12:25; (4) Isaiah 41:10; 43:1–3; (5) Jeremiah 32:17; (6) Matthew 6:25–34; (7) John 14:1–6, 27; 16:33; (8) Romans 5:3–5; 8:31–39; (9) Philippians 4:6–7; (10) 2 Timothy 1:7; (11) Hebrews 13:6; (12) 1 Peter 5:6–7

Resources

Dan B. Allender and Tremper Longman III, *Breaking the Idols of Your Heart*
Dan B. Allender and Tremper Longman III, *The Cry of the Soul*
Jerry Bridges, *Respectable Sins*
Gary R. Collins, *Christian Counseling*, chaps. 8–11, 18
Robert D. Jones, *Forgiveness*
David Powlison, *Good and Angry*
David Powlison, *Stress*
David Powlison, *Worry*
Barbara Raveling, *The Renewing of the Mind Project*
Edward T. Welch, *Depression*
Edward T. Welch, *"Just One More"*
Edward T. Welch, *Shame Interrupted*
Edward T. Welch, *When I Am Afraid*
Edward T. Welch, *When People Are Big and God Is Small*

71. How do you maintain healthy friendships?

Friendships can be wonderful and deeply painful. As you review the following texts of Scripture in their contexts, look for elements of true friendship, and try to discern what went wrong when there were problems.

(1) Exodus 33:11; (2) Isaiah 41:8; James 2:23; (3) 1 Samuel 30:26; (4) 2 Samuel 15–17;[52] (5) Psalm 38:11; (6) Psalm 41:9; (7) Psalm 55:12–14, 20–21; (8) Proverbs 17:17; (9) Proverbs 18:24; (10) Proverbs 14:20; 19:4–7; (11) Proverbs 27:6, 9–10; (12) Luke 11:5–8; (13) John 11:11; (14) Acts 13:1; (15) Esther 5:14; (16) Job 2:11; 16:20; 19:14, 19; (17) Job 42:10; (18) Proverbs 16:28; (19) Proverbs 17:9; (20) Proverbs 22:24; (21) Jeremiah 20:10; 38:22; (22) Lamentations 1:2; (23) Mark 5:19; (24) Luke 14:12; (25) Luke 15:6, 9, 29; (26) Luke 21:16; (27) Luke 23:12; (28) John 15:13–15; (29) Acts 10:24; (30) Acts 19:31; (31) Acts 24:23; 27:3

52. Notice what the text says about Hushai, David's friend.

Resources

Dee Brestin, *The Friendships of Women*
Jonathan Holmes, *The Company We Keep*
Christine Hoover, *Messy Beautiful Friendship*
Vaughan Roberts, *True Friendship*
Edward T. Welch, *Side by Side*

72. How do you rebuke or admonish people?

(1) Psalm 141:5; **(2)** Proverbs 3:11; 13:1; 17:10; **(3)** Proverbs 27:5; 28:23; **(4)** 1 Timothy 5:1; **(5)** 1 Timothy 5:20; **(6)** 2 Timothy 4:2; **(7)** Titus 1:9, 13; 2:15; **(8)** Matthew 18:15; **(9)** 2 Corinthians 10:1; **(10)** Colossians 1:28; **(11)** Psalm 81:8; **(12)** Luke 17:3; **(13)** Luke 23:40; **(14)** Acts 20:31; **(15)** 1 Corinthians 4:14; **(16)** Colossians 3:16; **(17)** 1 Thessalonians 5:12; **(18)** 1 Thessalonians 5:14; **(19)** Revelation 3:19; **(20)** Galatians 6:1

Resources

David Powlison, *Speaking Truth in Love*
Paul David Tripp, *Instruments in the Redeemer's Hands*

73. How do you teach the Bible?

(1) 1 Corinthians 4:1–5; **(2)** 2 Corinthians 4:1–6; **(3)** Acts 17:1–3, 17, 22–31; **(4)** Colossians 4:3–4; **(5)** 1 Corinthians 14:9; **(6)** Ephesians 6:18–20; **(7)** Philippians 1:9–11; **(8)** 2 Corinthians 1:13;[53] **(9)** 2 Corinthians 2:17; **(10)** 2 Timothy 3:16–17

Resources

Jonathan Leeman, *Word-Centered Church*
Greg Scharf, *Let the Earth Hear His Voice*
Trevin Wax, *Gospel-Centered Teaching*

74. How do you nurture your children for Christ?

(1) Deuteronomy 4:9; 6:1–9, 20–25; 11:18–21; 32:7; **(2)** Psalm 44:1; **(3)** Joshua 24:14–15; **(4)** Psalm 34:8–14; **(5)** Psalm 128; **(6)** Proverbs 1:1–7; 4:1–27; 13:22; 22:6;

53. What was Paul's standard for the level of comprehension he aimed for?

(7) Matthew 28:18–20; **(8)** 1 Corinthians 4:14–16; 11:1; **(9)** Philippians 3:17; 4:9; **(10)** 1 Timothy 4:12; **(11)** Ephesians 6:1–4; **(12)** Colossians 3:21; **(13)** 1 Thessalonians 2:11–12; **(14)** 1 Timothy 5:8; **(15)** 2 Timothy 3:10–17; **(16)** Hebrews 10:24–25; **(17)** Hebrews 12:5–11

Resources

Voddie Baucham Jr., *Family Driven Faith*
William P. Farley, *Gospel-Powered Parenting*
Starr Meade, *Give Them Truth*
Paul David Tripp, *Parenting*
Donald S. Whitney, *Family Worship*

75. How would you articulate a robust Christian worldview?

As believers, we want to be so saturated by the perspective of the Bible that we can engage with any aspect of life in a way that honors Christ. This ability to think Christianly about an issue is sometimes called "having a Christian worldview."

In a way, this entire training process has been striving to give you such a worldview—by immersing you in Scripture and challenging you to connect God's truth with the realities of life. In this final question, we focus your attention on a variety of cultural issues that you may encounter as elders but that are not explicitly addressed or completely unpacked in the Bible. A faithful and robust Christian worldview will allow you to process such issues faithfully and lead God's people well.

So how does a Christian worldview actually function?

If you are going to evaluate a cultural issue so you can remain true to the Lord, consider what is necessary:

1. Your mind must be molded by God's truth. Certain core biblical doctrines—especially relevant to cultural issues—must be kept close at hand. These will, of course, shape your mind to align with God's perspective; but more relevant here, they will guard

your mind from coming to conclusions that are not aligned with God's perspective.

2. Your mind must use a biblical process to evaluate the cultural issue at hand. There must be a framework through which you can run an idea, institution, value, or concept—and which allows you to identify if and how it diverges from God's design and intention.

Both of these are necessary: you need relevant, biblical doctrines (which form the guardrails for truth) and a biblically shaped process (which guides into truth). In this question, you will work on both of these elements.

Biblical Guardrails

First, identify a variety of core doctrines that are especially important for Christians to have in mind when considering cultural issues. Note that these doctrines flow from systematic theology. Use the verses below to explore key doctrinal truths that guard a Christian worldview.

General revelation

(1) Psalms 8:1–9; 19:1–4a; **(2)** Romans 1:19–20; **(3)** Matthew 5:45b; **(4)** Luke 6:35b; **(5)** Acts 14:15–17; 17:24–27

Special revelation

(1) Deuteronomy 29:29; **(2)** Psalms 19:7–11; 119:1–8; **(3)** Romans 15:4; **(4)** 1 Corinthians 10:11–12; **(5)** 2 Timothy 3:14–17; **(6)** Hebrews 4:12–13; **(7)** 2 Peter 2:16–21

God's greatness and glory

(1) 1 Chronicles 29:10–13; **(2)** Psalms 24:1–2; 135:6; **(3)** Romans 11:33–36

God's good vision for life in the garden

(1) Genesis 1:4, 10, 12, 18, 21, 25, 31; (2) Genesis 1:26–27

The effect and extent of sin

(1) Genesis 3:1–19; (2) Jeremiah 17:9; (3) Romans 3:10–18, 23; 7:14–24; (4) James 2:10; 4:17; (5) 1 John 1:8, 10

The supremacy and perfection of Christ

(1) Colossians 1:15–20; (2) Hebrews 1:1–4; (3) John 1:1–4, 14, 18

The effect of Christ's work—on human souls, on creation, on history

(1) John 3:14–18; 14:6; (2) Romans 8:19–23; (3) Revelation 21:5–8; 22:7, 12–15; (4) Revelation 21:1–22:5

A Biblical Process

Second, consider the following biblical framework that you can use to evaluate how a cultural issue fits into God's design for the world.[54] Note that this framework flows from biblical theology.[55]

1. *Primitive integrity.* What was God's design for the world? What was life like before the fall, when God was honored as King, relationships were as God intended, and humans lived according to God's ways?

   (a) Genesis 1:1; (b) Psalm 24:1; (c) Isaiah 40:28; (d) Nehemiah 9:6; (e) Genesis 2:18–25; (f) Genesis 3:8; (g) Genesis 1:28–30; 2:15–17; (h) Genesis 2:7; (i) Psalm 103:14

---

54. This framework is from Thomas Boston (1676–1732), *Human Nature in Its Fourfold State* (repr. Edinburgh, UK: Banner of Truth Trust, 2015).

55. For those unfamiliar with the distinctions, biblical theology describes theology as it develops through Scripture. It looks "down the line" of Scripture and asks, Where is this idea or theme going? Systematic theology breaks up theology into different topics and examines them separately. It looks "across the grain" and asks, What is the summary understanding of this doctrine?

2. *Entire depravity.* How has sin affected the relationship between humans and God, humans and themselves, humans and other humans, and humans and the created world?

> (a) Genesis 3:7–19; (b) Romans 1:18–32; (c) Ephesians 2:1–3; (d) 2 Corinthians 4:4; (e) John 5:39–40; 8:34; (f) John 3:19; (g) Romans 8:7; (h) 2 Timothy 3:2–9; (i) Ephesians 4:18; (j) Romans 3:9–20; 8:18–23

3. *Begun recovery.* How does a person's relationship with Christ begin a process of reversing the effects and extent of sin? How much completed transformation can we expect while we are still in this sinful world, in a body still touched by sin, and contending with a sinful nature that still haunts us even though it no longer reigns in us?

> (a) Ephesians 2:4–10; (b) Romans 12:1–2; (c) 2 Corinthians 4:6; (d) Jeremiah 31:31–34; (e) Ezekiel 36:25–27; (f) 1 Peter 1:8; (g) Romans 6:6–23; (h) Galatians 5:1; (i) John 16:8–11; (j) Romans 8:1–17; (k) Ephesians 4:17–6:4; (l) Galatians 5:16–25; (m) Ephesians 6:10–18; (n) 1 Peter 5:8–11; (o) 1 John 1:8–2:2; (p) Ephesians 1:14; (q) Philippians 3:20–21; (r) 1 Thessalonians 1:9–10; (s) Titus 2:11–13; (t) Romans 8:12–17, 22–25

4. *The consummation of all things.* What does Jesus promise for our eternity, when he returns to set all things right?

> (a) Matthew 25:46; (b) 2 Corinthians 5:1–5; (c) 1 Corinthians 15:20–58; (d) 1 John 3:1–3; (e) 1 Corinthians 13:12; (f) Revelation 19:1–8; 19:22–22:5; (g) Romans 8:18–25

Cultural Issues to Evaluate

A Christian worldview will enable you to process current cultural issues and temptations so that you can respond in ways that honor God, reflect his wisdom, promote his kingdom, and maintain faithfulness to the Bible. At a pace appropriate for you and your group, seek to think and act Christianly about the matters listed below. These texts often address issues only somewhat related to the cultural issue being explored. The texts listed with each issue clarify Scripture's assessment of the behavior, attitude, or practice.

Abortion

(1) Exodus 21:22–25; (2) Job 31:15; (3) Psalms 22:10; 127:3–5; 139:13–16; (4) Jeremiah 1:5; (5) Luke 1:42–45; (6) Galatians 1:15

Addiction to various substances and practices

(1) Jeremiah 2:23–25; (2) John 8:34; (3) Proverbs 20:1; (4) 1 Corinthians 10:13; (5) Galatians 5:1, 16–25; 6:1–2; (6) Colossians 3:5–17; (7) 1 Peter 2:11–12; (8) 2 Peter 2:19

Adultery

(1) Exodus 20:14; (2) Leviticus 18:20; 20:10; (3) Deuteronomy 22:22–24; (4) Proverbs 2:16–19; 6:20–35; (5) Jeremiah 23:10–15; 29:20–23; (6) Matthew 5:27–30; 19:3–9; (7) Hebrews 13:4

Assisted suicide and suicide

(1) 1 Samuel 31:1–7; (2) Judges 9:50–57; 16:21–31; (3) 2 Samuel 17:23; (4) 1 Kings 16:15–20; (5) Matthew 27:3–5; (6) Acts 1:15–18; (7) Genesis 9:6; (8) Exodus 20:13; (9) Job 1:20–22; 2:9–10; 7:13–16; 33:4; (10) Psalms 31:15; 34:17–20; (11) Ecclesiastes 3:1–3; 7:17; 8:7–8

Dating and marriage to a non-Christian

(1) Deuteronomy 7:1–4; (2) Ezra 9:1–10:5; (3) 1 Corinthians 2:14; 7:12–14, 39; (4) 2 Corinthians 6:14–15

Divorce and remarriage after divorce

(1) Genesis 2:24; (2) Exodus 21:9–11; (3) Deuteronomy 24:1–4; (4) Proverbs 5:18; (5) Jeremiah 3:1; (6) Malachi 2:14–16; (7) Matthew 5:31–32; 19:1–12; (8) Mark 10:1–12; (9) Luke 16:18; (10) Romans 7:2–3; (11) 1 Corinthians 7:10–16, 39

Environmentalism

(1) Genesis 1:26–31; 2:15–20a; 3:17; 9:1–11; (2) Deuteronomy 20:19–20; (3) Psalm 24:1–2; (4) Hosea 4:1–3; (5) Romans 8:19–22; (6) Isaiah 11:1–9; 35:1–10; 55:12–13; (7) Revelation 22:1–2; (8) 2 Peter 3:11–13

Gambling and the motives that may underlie it

(1) Exodus 20:17; (2) Proverbs 13:11; (3) Ecclesiastes 5:10; (4) Matthew 6:19–21, 24; (5) Mark 8:36; (6) Luke 12:15; (7) 1 Timothy 6:6–11, 17–19; (8) Hebrews 13:5; (9) Ephesians 4:14;[56] (10) Ephesians 4:28

Genetic engineering and transhumanism

(1) Genesis 1:26–31; 2:7–9; 11:1–9; (2) Ecclesiastes 7:13; (3) Psalm 139:13–16; (4) Romans 1:18–25; (5) 1 Corinthians 6:19–20; 15:38–39; (6) Ephesians 5:29; (7) Philippians 3:21; (8) Colossians 1:16; (9) 1 Timothy 4:4

Human trafficking

(1) Genesis 1:26–27; (2) Deuteronomy 24:7; (3) Psalm 82:4; (4) Proverbs 31:8–9; (5) Isaiah 58:6–7; (6) Isaiah 61:1–3, 8a; (7) Zechariah 7:10; (8) 1 Timothy 1:8–11; (9) James 1:27

Immigration and refugees

(1) Exodus 12:49; 22:21; (2) Leviticus 19:33–34; 24:22; (3) Deuteronomy 1:16; 6:10–13; 10:18–19; 24:14–18; (4) 1 Chronicles 29:14–15; (5) Isaiah 16:3–5; (6) Jeremiah 7:5–7; 22:3–5; (7) Romans 13:1; (8) Hebrews 13:1–2; (9) 1 Peter 2:11–17

Indebtedness

(1) Deuteronomy 28:44; (2) Psalm 37:21; (3) Proverbs 3:27–28; 6:1–5; 17:18; 22:26–27; (4) Proverbs 22:7; (5) Nehemiah 5:2–4; (6) Romans 13:8; (7) Deuteronomy 15:1–11

Military service

(1) Deuteronomy 20:1–20; (2) Joshua 11; (3) 2 Samuel 11; (4) Psalms 33:12–22; 144:1–2; (5) Ecclesiastes 3:8; (6) Isaiah 2:1–4; (7) Matthew 5:38–42; (8) John 15:13; (9) Romans 12:17–13:7; (10) 1 Timothy 2:1–4; (11) 2 Timothy 2:1–7; (12) 1 Peter 2:21–25; (13) Luke 3:14

---

56. Note that the word translated "craftiness" literally means "dice playing." Gambling and cheating were closely associated.

Multiculturalism

(1) Deuteronomy 12:29–32; (2) Matthew 28:18–20; (3) John 10:7–16; 14:6; (4) Acts 6:1–7;[57] 13:1–3; (5) Ephesians 2:11–22; (6) Acts 4:12; 17:22–31; (7) Romans 1:16–17; (8) 1 Corinthians 9:19–23; 10:31–11:1; (9) Galatians 3:27–28; (10) Revelation 7:9–10

Public, private, or home school

(1) Deuteronomy 6:4–9, 20–25; 11:19; (2) Proverbs 1:7–9; 2:1–5; 4:1–5;[58] (3) John 17:14–17; (4) Matthew 11:29; (5) Romans 14:1–23; (6) 1 Corinthians 10:23–33; 15:33; (7) Ephesians 6:1–4; (8) 2 Timothy 3:14–17; (9) 1 Peter 2:11–12; (10) 1 Corinthians 10:23–33

Questions surrounding creation

(1) Genesis 1:1–2:4; (2) Exodus 20:11; 31:17; (3) Job 38:1–7; (4) Psalms 19:1–4; 33:8–9; 104:5; 148:5–6; (5) Isaiah 40:28; 44:24; 45:12, 18; (6) John 1:1–3; (7) Romans 1:19–20; 4:17; 14:1–23; (8) Colossians 1:16; (9) Hebrews 11:3; (10) 2 Peter 3:5, 8; (11) Revelation 4:11; 10:6

Racism

(1) Genesis 1:26–27; (2) 1 Samuel 16:7; (3) Proverbs 22:2; (4) Matthew 28:18–20; (5) John 3:16; 13:34; (6) Acts 10:28; (7) Romans 2:11; 3:9, 22–23; 10:12–13; 12:3, 9–16; (8) Galatians 3:26–28; (9) Ephesians 2:11–22; (10) Colossians 3:11; (11) James 2:8–9; (12) 1 John 2:7–11; 3:11–15; 4:19–21; (13) Revelation 7:9–10

Same-sex practice[59]

(1) Genesis 2:18–24; 19:1–29; (2) Leviticus 18:22; 20:13; (3) Judges 19:22–26; (4) Matthew 19:3–12; (5) Romans 1:18–32; (6) 1 Corinthians 5:9–13; 6:9–20; (7) 1 Timothy 1:8–11; (8) 1 John 3:4–10; (9) Jude 7

---

57. Consider the negative effects of ethnic favoritism.
58. This theme also runs throughout Proverbs.
59. Same-sex practice describes those who embrace and actively engage in same-sex activity. It is well worth your time to consider the way a Christian worldview helps you understand same-sex attraction and same-sex marriage, two related but independent issues.

Social drinking

(1) Psalm 104:14–15; (2) Proverbs 3:9–10; 20:1; 23:29–35; (3) Isaiah 5:11, 22; 28:7–8; 55:1; (4) Hosea 4:11; (5) John 2:1–11; (6) Romans 14:13–23; (7) 1 Corinthians 8:8–13; 10:23–11:1; (8) Galatians 5:21; (9) Ephesians 5:18–20; (10) 1 Timothy 3:8; 4:3–5; 5:23; (11) Titus 2:3; (12) 1 Peter 4:1–5; 5:8

Social media and technology

(1) Genesis 11:4–6; (2) Micah 5:13; (3) Psalm 20:7; (4) 1 Corinthians 6:12; 10:23; (5) Ephesians 4:29; (6) Colossians 3:16; (7) 1 Thessalonians 5:11; (8) Hebrews 3:13; 10:24–25; (9) James 4:4; (10) 2 Peter 2:19; (11) 1 John 4:1

Transgenderism

(1) Exodus 20:17; (2) Genesis 1:26–28; 2:18–24; (3) Deuteronomy 22:5; (4) Matthew 19:11–12; (5) Romans 1:18–32; (6) James 4:2

Resources

Craig G. Bartholomew and Michael W. Goheen, *The Drama of Scripture*
J. Daryl Charles, ed., *Reading Genesis 1–2*
Gary R. Collins, *Christian Counseling*, chaps. 19, 21, 27, 30, 32, 34–36
Charles Colson and Nancy Pearcey, *How Now Shall We Live?*
Andy Crouch, *Culture Making*
Andy Crouch, *The Tech-Wise Family*
Howard L. Dayton, *Your Money Counts*
Kevin DeYoung, *What Does the Bible Really Teach about Homosexuality?*
Michael Emerson and Christian Smith, *Divided by Faith*
John S. Feinberg and Paul D. Feinberg, *Ethics for a Brave New World*
James K. Hoffmeier, *The Immigration Crisis*
John F. Kilner, ed., *Why the Church Needs Bioethics*
Andreas J. Köstenberger and David W. Jones, *God, Marriage, and Family*
Martin Luther, *Christians Can Be Soldiers*
Trillia J. Newbell, *United*
Tony Reinke, *12 Ways Your Phone Is Changing You*
Vaughn Roberts, *God's Big Picture*
Vaughn Roberts, *Talking Points*
R. C. Sproul, *Abortion*
John R. W. Stott, *Same Sex Relationships*
Edward T. Welch, *Addictions*
Albert M. Wolters, *Creation Regained*
Christopher J. H. Wright, *The Mission of God's People*, chap. 3

PART 3

TWO ADDITIONAL DISCIPLESHIP RESOURCES

7

Learning to Follow Jesus

A Thematic Resource for Discipling Others

This chapter is for anyone wanting a tool for discipling someone else. I (Greg) wrote it for those whom I was discipling individually. It was long my practice to prayerfully seek to disciple three men every academic year. I hoped that one of these would be a new Christian and another would be an emerging leader. I used this material with all sorts of people, but with different instructions. For the new believer, this served as a basic introduction to the Christian life; for the emerging leader, it was a tool I was teaching them by example to use in their own discipling ministry. I also used all sorts of other material, including "BA (Biblical Agenda) in Christian Living," the study of 2 Peter that is included in the next chapter, and you can use them as the Lord leads. You may prefer to write your own materials and may even do so in connection with a sermon series. As a pastor I mainly practiced consecutive exposition of biblical books, so I did not preach through the material in this chapter (I did use the study of 2 Peter in chapter 8 as the basis for a sermon series). Whatever your situation, this resource will put one more arrow in your quiver as you work at making disciples. Feel free to expand or contract it to suit the needs of the individual you are prayerfully discipling.

So it does not matter whether you are giving basic instruction to a new believer, offering a refresher course for an established believer, or modeling how to cover the basics of Christian living so an emerging leader has a framework for discipling someone else. The aim of this material is to get the other person to look at biblical texts that address what all growing Christians need. The repetition of the word "learning" underscores that a disciple is a learner—an apprentice, if you will, someone who learns by doing.

Overview

1. Learning to Eat
2. Learning to Walk (in the Spirit)
3. Learning to Talk (to God)
4. Learning to Trust Your (Heavenly) Father
5. Learning to Love the Family and Others
6. Learning to Sacrifice
7. Learning to Serve
8. Learning to Fight the Enemy
9. Learning to Bring Others into the Family
10. Learning to Use Your Birthday Presents
11. Learning to Think like an Adult
12. Learning to See the World as God Sees It
13. Learning to Handle Hard Times

Before You Begin: Steps in Bible Study

The fact that this study is topical in nature does not give license to disregard basic principles of biblical interpretation or to take passages out of context. Here are just a few such principles that none of us can afford to ignore.

1. Decide what passage to study. In this resource, you will be directed toward a biblical passage. When you are studying on your own, it is important to remember to study passages that are at least a thought unit. Words and phrases only have meaning in sentences, and these can only be properly understood in paragraphs. In narrative texts, look for the beginning and end of the story, and read the whole thing; in poetry, read the whole poem; in prophecy, read the whole oracle.

2. Pray for the Spirit's illumination and for your own willingness to obey. God wants you to understand his Word so that you can respond to it in ways that the Word itself suggests or states. Because he gave us his Word for our good, we can count on him to help us see what is actually there when we read it. Praying for illumination is asking God, by his indwelling Spirit, to turn the light on as we look at the pages of Scripture. He delights to answer this prayer. Nevertheless, he wants us to see what he put there so we can believe what he tells us and do what he requires of us. If we are unwilling to obey, we should not complain if we do not understand. Ask God to help you to see and be willing to obey what you see.

3. Read the passage alertly, observantly, and repeatedly. An often-neglected step in careful Bible study is simply reading the passage in an accurate, clear translation. Consider reading the English Standard Version (ESV) or the Christian Standard Bible (CSB) or another comparatively literal English translation of the Bible. If you are an oral/aural learner, you may find it helpful to read the passage aloud; you may hear things you did not catch when you read. And read or listen to it multiple times; almost all of us see things on the third or fourth reading that we missed earlier.

4. Consider the words used. All Scripture is God-breathed. That means that every word counts; none is there by accident. Godly, careful, gifted, trained scholars have rendered the original languages into

our language so that a careful reading of the English translation will almost never lead you astray. (If you can learn the original tongues, by all means do so. You will see things you might miss otherwise, but this is by no means required for fruitful Bible study.)

5. Pay attention to the grammar and syntax. Blessed are you if a teacher taught you enough grammar to help you understand how the inspired words of the biblical text work together to say and do what God designed them to do. For instance, if you know the difference between an independent clause and a dependent one, you are well on your way to distinguishing main ideas of passages from supporting ideas.

6. Notice the context. Context is king, as the saying goes. Every word, every phrase, every sentence adds something to what is around it. Each part is there for a purpose, and we can only discover that purpose by studying each part of a passage in its wider context. So work outward, as it were, in concentric circles from the part you are studying to see the bigger picture and what your part is contributing to that larger whole. The whole Bible is a drama of redemption, the story of how God gets glory for himself by the creation, despite the fall, by purchasing our redemption, and ultimately in the consummation of all things. Every part of the Bible in some way fits into this story line. The more you know the parts, the clearer the whole will become, and vice versa.

7. Let the other passages help you understand the one you are studying. No passage can mean what a clearer text elsewhere plainly contradicts, and other passages often shed light on the one you are studying. Sometimes they qualify or limit it; sometimes they particularize a general statement or generalize a particular instance. Cross-references in your study Bible or center or margin notes are a good starting place to discover these other texts. A concordance can also be a great help in discovering parallel passages, but beware of assuming that the same word is talking about the same thing in a different context.

8. Summarize the thrust of the passage. Much misunderstanding occurs when a reader elevates a secondary or supportive idea to the status of the main idea of a passage. Train yourself, through practice, to discern the main thing the author is saying. Once you see that clearly, all of the other ideas in the passage will more readily take their rightful places explaining, expanding, qualifying, applying, or otherwise relating to that dominant idea. This is an especially important discipline if you are tasked with teaching the passage.

9. Check your conclusions by consulting other sources. Once you have done your own careful study, it often pays to look at study Bible notes, quality commentaries, or other reference tools, such as the Scripture index of a good systematic theology. These are no substitute for doing your own careful study, but if you have access to such aids, thank God and let others point out things they have learned.

10. Respond to the truth you have discovered. No Bible study is complete until we respond with faith and obedience to what we have read. Appropriate responses are dictated by the passage itself. Second Timothy 3:16 lists the four most basic reasons God breathed out the Bible. If your text is "teaching," then understanding and belief are appropriate responses. If it is "rebuking," let the passage tell you what sin you need to confess and repent of. If the text is mainly "correcting," take the way of obedience it provides. If it is "training for righteousness," let it equip you in any number of ways so that you may be thoroughly prepared for every good work. When you respond in ways that God designed the text to foster, he will delight to keep feeding you with his Word and so transform you into the likeness of Christ.

General Instructions

These thirteen lessons aim to help you take steps toward learning the Christian life skill indicated in the title. In each case, much more could be said. Indeed, disciples of any level of maturity are still growing into each of these. These lessons are merely a first few baby steps related to each developmental milestone. Doing the exercise will not produce mastery of the skill addressed, but it should be a valuable review for the more seasoned Christian and a helpful introduction for new believers. Feel free to consult other resources as time and availability dictate and to slow the pace if repetition is called for.

1. Learning to Eat

Passages: Read each of these in context, noting what it contributes to the context. Try to draw valid inferences from what each text says.

(1) 1 Peter 2:2–3; (2) Hebrews 5:11–14; (3) 1 Corinthians 3:1–3; (4) Psalm 119:103; (5) Psalm 141:4; (6) Jeremiah 15:16

Diet: What are you able to eat and assimilate? Milk? Baby food? Meat?

Develop an appetite: "Try it, you'll like it." Active, growing kids need more to eat.

How to actually devour the Bible: The Navigators' "hand" illustration concerning how one gets a grip on God's Word. Try to pick up your Bible using only the little finger of one hand, representing hearing the Word. It is not easy. Adding the ring finger, representing reading and grasping the Word, helps, but only slightly. Study, the middle finger, is better but your grip is still precarious. The index finger, memorizing, is even more helpful, but it is the thumb, representing meditating on the Word, that actually helps us get a grip on Scripture. Add the thumb to any of the other fingers and there is some level of grip; put them all together and you have a meaningful grip on the Bible.

Hear. Deuteronomy 31:12–13; Hebrews 3:7–8

Read. Deuteronomy 17:19

Study. Psalm 119:45, 94 (CSB)[1]

Memorize. Psalm 119:11, 52

Meditate. Joshua 1:8; Psalm 119:15, 23, 27, 48, 54–55, 99

How should we read the Bible?

(1) Psalm 119:18, 34, 66; **(2)** Psalm 119:58; **(3)** Psalm 119:17, 33–34, 100

When and where should we do it?

Develop a habit.

Set a goal.

Keep a notebook.

Follow a plan.

Vary your speed.

Remove distractions, noise, and clutter.

Allow enough time to digest.

Read the passage more than once.

Use a Bible dictionary, concordance, and cross-references to help you understand the passage.

Ask what the passage is getting at, and summarize its thrust in your own words.

Let the context help you grasp the meaning.

Assignment: Write your own goal for eating God's Word this week.

Consider reading *A Hunger for God* by John Piper.[2]

---

1. The Hebrew that the CSB translates "study" (v. 45) and "studied" (v. 94) is more literally "sought out" (cf. ESV).

2. John Piper, *A Hunger for God: Desiring God through Fasting and Prayer* (Wheaton: Crossway, 2013).

2. Learning to Walk (in the Spirit)

Passages: Read each of these in context, noting what it contributes to the context. Try to draw valid inferences from what each text says.

Who is the Holy Spirit?

(1) John 14:16–20; (2) Acts 1:4–5, 8; (3) Acts 2:4, 17; (4) Acts 5:3–4; (5) Matthew 28:19–20

What ministries does the Spirit have with the believer?

(1) John 3:5; (2) Titus 3:5–6; (3) Ephesians 1:13–14; (4) 1 Corinthians 12:13; (5) Romans 8:16; (6) Romans 8:25–27; (7) John 7:37–39; (8) Acts 1:8; (9) 1 Corinthians 2:9–13; (10) 1 Corinthians 3:16

How are we filled with the Holy Spirit?

Ephesians 5:14–18

What does it mean to walk in the Spirit or keep in step with the Spirit?

(1) Galatians 5:13–26; (2) Ephesians 4:30–32; (3) 1 Thessalonians 5:19; (4) Acts 7:51

Assignment:

1. Remember to feed on God's Word daily. How many meals did you have last week? How many snacks? How many days did you go spiritually hungry and thirsty?

2. List one or two steps of obedience that you know the Spirit is urging you to take.

3. Ask the Spirit to help you obey and to put to death the urge to do the opposite (a work of the flesh). Take the step of obedience, trusting God to help you.

Consider reading *Keep in Step with the Spirit* by J. I. Packer.[3]

---

3. J. I. Packer, *Keep in Step with the Spirit: Finding Fullness in Our Walk with God*, rev. ed. (Grand Rapids: Baker Books, 2005).

3. Learning to Talk (to God)

Passages: Read each of these in context, noting what it contributes to the context. Try to draw valid inferences from what each text says.

(1) Romans 8:15–17; (2) Luke 11:1–13

What are potential problems in prayer?

(1) James 4:2–3; (2) Psalm 66:18–19; (3) Isaiah 59:2; (4) Proverbs 1:23–28; (5) Proverbs 21:13; (6) James 1:6–7; (7) Luke 18:11–14; (8) Matthew 6:5–8; (9) John 15:7

What things keep you from praying? Be specific.

Ask God to help you overcome one of these this week. What can you do to avoid being hindered by that obstacle?

Obedience check: How did it go this week?

How is your appetite? Don't let Bible reading become any more of a burden than eating is! Just make it a regular part of your schedule. Vary your diet so it doesn't get boring.

Consider reading *Praying Backwards* by Bryan Chapell.[4]

4. Learning to Trust Your (Heavenly) Father

What is faith? It is not optimism that things will work out, not mere credence and docility in believing what the church says one should believe, but credence plus commitment.

> Faith is not just *fides* (credence) but, rather *fiducia* (confident trust).
> —J. I. Packer, *18 Words*

4. Bryan Chapell, *Praying Backwards: Transform Your Prayer Life by Beginning in Jesus' Name* (Grand Rapids: Baker Books, 2005).

> Saving faith is the hand of the soul . . . [which] grasps . . . and is saved. Saving faith is the eye of the soul. . . . [It] looks and is healed. Saving faith is the mouth of the soul. The sinner receives it, and is made well and strong. Saving faith is the foot of the soul. The sinner runs [to Jesus] and is safe.
>
> —J. C. Ryle, "Justification!"

What are the objects of faith? Read each text carefully and look for distinctions between them.

(1) Romans 4:24; **(2)** 1 Peter 1:21; **(3)** Romans 3:22–26; **(4)** Romans 4:20–21; **(5)** 1 John 5:1; **(6)** Romans 10:9; **(7)** Mark 1:15; **(8)** 2 Thessalonians 1:10

What is the source of faith?

(1) Titus 1:2; **(2)** 2 Samuel 7:28; **(3)** Psalm 12:6; **(4)** Psalm 9:10; **(5)** 1 John 5:10; **(6)** 1 Thessalonians 2:13; **(7)** Romans 10:15–17; **(8)** Ephesians 2:8–9

What are some counterfeits of biblical faith?

Legalism

Ritualism

"Principle-ism" (i.e., trusting a principle from God instead of trusting God himself)

Moralism

Gnosticism

Check-up: All people live by faith. The difference lies in the object of faith. Even believers are tempted to place their ultimate trust in things, people, ideas, and accomplishments—anything other than Christ. To some extent, we can detect this sort of idolatry by asking how we would feel if the following were removed: family, job, bank account, health, political freedom, reputation, academic degrees, Christian service, appearance, mental health.

What or whom are you trusting?

Consider reading *How People Change* by Timothy Lane and Paul David Tripp.[5]

Review: Has your diet been balanced this week? Have you said "yes" to the Holy Spirit? What have you and the Father talked about?

5. Learning to Love the Family and Others

Passages: Read each of these in context, noting what it contributes to the context. Try to draw valid inferences from what each text says.

What does Jesus teach about love?

> **(1)** Matthew 5:43–46; **(2)** Matthew 19:19; **(3)** Matthew 22:37–40; **(4)** John 13:34–35

What is Jesus's example?

> **(1)** John 13:3–17; **(2)** Luke 23:34

What do the Epistles teach?

> **(1)** Romans 12:9–10, 20; **(2)** Romans 13:8–10; **(3)** 1 Corinthians 13; **(4)** 1 Corinthians 16:14; **(5)** Galatians 5:6, 13–14, 22; **(6)** Ephesians 1:15; **(7)** Ephesians 4:2; **(8)** Ephesians 4:15–16; **(9)** Ephesians 5:2, 25, 33; **(10)** Philippians 2:2–4; **(11)** 1 Thessalonians 4:9; **(12)** 1 Thessalonians 5:13; **(13)** 2 Timothy 1:7; **(14)** Titus 2:4; **(15)** Hebrews 6:10; **(16)** Hebrews 10:24; **(17)** Hebrews 13:1; **(18)** James 2:8; **(19)** 1 Peter 1:22; **(20)** 1 Peter 2:17; **(21)** 1 John 3:11, 18, 23; **(22)** 1 John 4:7–12; **(23)** 1 John 4:16–21; **(24)** 1 John 5:1

How do we learn to love?

How are we called to love?

How can you show love best to those around you?

5. Timothy S. Lane and Paul David Tripp, *How People Change* (Greensboro, NC: New Growth, 2006).

Consider reading *The Mark of Jesus* by Timothy George and John Woodbridge.[6]

6. Learning to Sacrifice

Passages: Read each of these in context, noting what it contributes to the context. Try to draw valid inferences from what each text says.

(1) Romans 12:1–2; **(2)** Luke 14:25–34[7]

Notice the excuses the people gave in Luke 14:18–19. What excuses are you tempted to make when the Lord calls on you to sacrifice for his kingdom?

When is a sacrifice no sacrifice at all?

(1) Philippians 3:7–11; **(2)** Matthew 13:44–45

What sacrifices is God asking you to make?

What might help you to joyfully make those sacrifices?

(1) 1 Peter 5:8–11; **(2)** Hebrews 10:32–34

Consider reading *Radical* by David Platt.[8]

7. Learning to Serve

Passages: Read each of these in context, noting what it contributes to the context. Try to draw valid inferences from what each text says.

---

6. Timothy George and John Woodbridge, *The Mark of Jesus: Loving in a Way the World Can See* (Chicago: Moody, 2005).

7. To whom is Jesus speaking? Notice three conditions of discipleship in verses 26, 27 (cf. Exod. 20:12 and 1 Tim. 5:8; "hate" in this context means "love less"), and 33.

8. David Platt, *Radical: Taking Back Your Faith from the American Dream* (Colorado Springs: Multnomah, 2010).

What is the pattern of our service?

(1) Matthew 10:24–25; **(2)** Philippians 2:6–7; **(3)** Matthew 23:11; 24:45–50; **(4)** Mark 10:44–45

What is the restriction on our service?

Luke 16:13

How does Paul exemplify service?

1 Corinthians 9:19

What will be the reward?

1 Kings 12:7

What characterizes a servant's attitude?

What alternatives to servanthood should be detected and rejected?

(1) Matthew 20:25; 2 Corinthians 1:24; **(2)** Luke 9:24; 14:26; **(3)** John 10:12–13; **(4)** Genesis 28:18–22; 2 Peter 2; 2 Timothy 3:4–5

How can we serve each other in our church?

How can we serve our community?

None of us is asked to do everything that the body of Christ as a whole is called to do. Ask the Lord to show you what you are to do as his servant.

Consider reading *Ordinary* by Michael Horton.[9]

---

9. Michael Horton, *Ordinary: Sustainable Faith in a Radical, Restless World* (Grand Rapids: Zondervan, 2014).

8. Learning to Fight the Enemy

Passages: Read each of these in context, noting what it contributes to the context. Try to draw valid inferences from what each text says.

Who are our enemies?

1. Satan
   (a) Matthew 4:5–11 (CSB); (b) John 8:44; (c) 1 Timothy 3:6; (d) Ephesians 2:2; (e) 1 John 2:13; (f) 1 Peter 5:8; (g) Revelation 12:9–10; (h) John 12:31

2. The world[10]
   (a) John 7:7; (b) John 8:23; (c) John 14:30; (d) 1 Corinthians 2:12; (e) Galatians 4:3; (f) Colossians 2:8; (g) James 1:27; (h) 1 John 2:16; (i) 1 John 5:19; (j) Titus 2:12

3. The flesh
   (a) 2 Peter 2:18; (b) Matthew 26:41; (c) Romans 8:4; (d) 1 Corinthians 5:5; (e) Galatians 6:8; (f) Colossians 2:18;[11] (g) 1 Peter 2:11; (h) 1 Corinthians 3:1, 3–4; (i) Romans 7:14; 8:13

What are our weapons?[12]

1. The cross and resurrection of Christ
   (a) Colossians 2:15; (b) Hebrews 2:14; (c) Revelation 12:11; (d) Galatians 6:14; (e) Colossians 2:13–15; 3:5–11

2. The Scriptures
   (a) Matthew 4:1–11; (b) Ephesians 6:10–17; (c) Psalm 119:9, 11

3. Prayer
   (a) James 4:7–10; (b) Ephesians 6:18; (c) 2 Corinthians 10:3–5; (d) Matthew 26:41

4. The Holy Spirit[13]
   (a) Galatians 5:13–26; 6:8; (b) Romans 8:13; (c) Zechariah 4:6

---

10. That is, unregenerate humanity in rebellion against God.
11. The word describing the mind is more literally "fleshly."
12. These weapons must be properly understood and not used superstitiously.
13. Numbers 4–7 are weapons in more general terms.

158

5. Fellowship

(a) Acts 2:42–47

6. The authority of Christ, our Captain

(a) Matthew 28:19–20; **(b)** Matthew 10:1; **(c)** Hebrews 2:10; **(d)** Hebrews 12:2; **(e)** Revelation 1:5; **(f)** Matthew 16:17–28; **(g)** Revelation 19:11–18

7. Baptism and the Lord's Supper

(a) Romans 6:1–4; **(b)** 1 Peter 3:21; **(c)** 1 Corinthians 11:23–32

What is our strategy?

(1) 2 Timothy 2:1–4; **(2)** Matthew 16:24; **(3)** James 4:7

Where is our confidence?

(1) Revelation 19:19–21; 20:7–10; **(2)** Revelation 11:15; also 18:1–19:21; **(3)** 1 John 3:2; **(4)** Philippians 3:20–21

Consider reading *Tempted and Tried* by Russell Moore.[14]

9. Learning to Bring Others into the Family

Why evangelize?

(1) Matthew 28:18–20; **(2)** Acts 1:8; **(3)** 1 Timothy 2:3–4; 2 Peter 3:9; **(4)** 1 Corinthians 9:16; **(5)** 2 Corinthians 5:14–20

Who is to be evangelized?

(1) John 3:16; **(2)** Mark 13:10

In what key ways is the message summarized?

(1) Matthew 4:23; **(2)** Mark 1:14–15; **(3)** Luke 4:43; **(4)** Matthew 13:19; **(5)** Acts 1:3; **(6)** Acts 8:12; **(7)** Acts 19:8–10; **(8)** Acts 20:25; **(9)** Acts 28:23; **(10)** Acts 28:31; **(11)** Acts 8:25; **(12)** Acts 14:6–7; **(13)** Acts 14:21–22; **(14)** Acts 15:7; **(15)** Acts 16:10; **(16)** Acts 20:24

14. Russell D. Moore, *Tempted and Tried: Temptation and the Triumph of Christ* (Wheaton: Crossway, 2011).

Put this good news of God's kingdom in your own words.

When we proclaim the good news to the spiritually dead, what may happen?

(1) Ephesians 2:1–10; **(2)** Matthew 10:14–15; **(3)** Matthew 10:16, 22

What does God give us as we proclaim the good news?

(1) Matthew 10:1; 28:18; **(2)** 2 Corinthians 5:20; **(3)** Acts 1:8; **(4)** John 16:8–11; **(5)** James 1:18; **(6)** John 12:32; **(7)** Colossians 1:28–29; **(8)** Ephesians 4:11–13

How do we actually do it?

(1) Colossians 4:2–4; **(2)** Colossians 4:5–6

Once we have prayed and lived lives that adorn the gospel before people in our community, we proclaim the good news to many people, in many ways. These include but are not limited to service-based evangelism, mass evangelism, targeted evangelism, stranger evangelism, friendship evangelism, cross-cultural evangelism, and hospitality evangelism. Sometimes telling the good news may feel to us like a discipline that we must undertake; sometimes it may feel like the natural overflow of our lives. It is always both a privilege and a responsibility.

Consider reading *Questioning Evangelism* by Randy Newman.[15]

10. Learning to Use Your Birthday Presents

What are spiritual gifts?

(1) 1 Corinthians 12:7; **(2)** 1 Peter 4:10 (NIV)

---

15. Randy Newman, *Questioning Evangelism: Engaging People's Hearts the Way Jesus Did*, 2nd ed. (Grand Rapids: Kregel, 2017).

> Our exercise of spiritual gifts is nothing more nor less than Christ himself ministering through his body to his body, to the Father and to all mankind.
>
> —J. I. Packer, *Keep in Step with the Spirit*

Who has them?

1 Corinthians 12:4–7

What are they used for?

1 Peter 4:10–11

Are any gifts unnecessary?

1 Corinthians 12:12–26, especially verse 22

How do I discover my spiritual gifts?

(1) Romans 12:4–8; **(2)** 1 Corinthians 12:4–6

Note: For spiritual gifts in the New Testament, remember your 4s and 12s: Ephesians 4; 1 Peter 4; Romans 12; 1 Corinthians 12.

Prayer: Ask God to show you.

Let the church tell you: Speak the truth in love.

Fruit: Are people built up when you exercise your gift?

Learn by experience: Some trial and error of ministries may be required.

How may spiritual gifts be classified?

(1) 1 Peter 4:11; **(2)** Ephesians 4:11

How does the Holy Spirit give gifts?

In Christ: 1 Corinthians 1:4–7

What gifts does he give?

(1) Ephesians 4:11; **(2)** Romans 12:6–8; **(3)** 1 Corinthians 12:7–11, 28–31

Are there dangers to beware of?

Spiritual pride

Disorderliness in worship

Classifying Christians as "charismatic" or "noncharismatic" when every true Christian has at least one gift, one charism

Consider reading *The Beginner's Guide to Spiritual Gifts* by Sam Storms.[16]

11. Learning to Think like an Adult

When I was a child, I talked like a child, I thought like a child, I reasoned like a child. When I became a man, I put the ways of childhood behind me.

—1 Cor. 13:11 NIV

The problem: Let these passages help you grasp the predicament. Notice symptoms of unregenerate, carnal, blinded, deceived, or immature thinking.

(1) Matthew 16:9; **(2)** John 12:40; **(3)** 1 Timothy 1:7; **(4)** 2 Corinthians 3:14; **(5)** 2 Corinthians 4:4; **(6)** 2 Corinthians 11:3; **(7)** Luke 24:25; **(8)** Galatians 3:1, 3; **(9)** 1 Timothy 6:9;[17] **(10)** Titus 3:3; **(11)** Luke 6:11;[18] **(12)** 2 Timothy 3:8–9; **(13)** Luke 1:51; **(14)** Ephesians 2:3; **(15)** Ephesians 4:18; **(16)** Colossians 1:21; **(17)** James 1:23–24

16. Sam Storms, *The Beginner's Guide to Spiritual Gifts*, 2nd ed. (Minneapolis: Bethany House, 2015).
17. "Senseless" (ESV) or "foolish" (NIV, CSB) is more literally "mindless."
18. "Fury" (ESV) or "furious" (NIV) means mindless rage toward Jesus (cf. CSB).

The solution: Let these texts remind you of God's provisions for us and perhaps suggest practical things we can do to get our minds thinking God's thoughts.

(1) Ephesians 3:4; **(2)** 2 Timothy 2:7; **(3)** Hebrews 11:3; **(4)** 2 Corinthians 10:4–5; **(5)** Philippians 4:7; **(6)** Romans 12:1–3, 16; **(7)** Matthew 22:37; **(8)** Ephesians 1:18; **(9)** Hebrews 8:10; **(10)** 1 Peter 1:13; **(11)** 2 Peter 3:1; **(12)** 1 John 5:20; **(13)** Hebrews 3:1; **(14)** Hebrews 10:24; **(15)** Luke 24:25; **(16)** Hebrews 6:1; **(17)** 2 Corinthians 3:5; **(18)** Romans 8:6–7, 27; **(19)** Romans 1:21–22; **(20)** 1 Corinthians 3:20

What are limits to our knowledge?

(1) Ephesians 3:20; **(2)** Romans 11:34; **(3)** 1 Corinthians 2:16; 13:12

Consider reading *Growing Your Faith* by Jerry Bridges.[19]

12. Learning to See the World as God Sees It

Developing a Christian worldview is not easy. What things can be hindrances?

(1) Ephesians 2:1–2; **(2)** 1 John 2:15–17; **(3)** Mark 7:8–13

A way of looking at God's world: four stages
1. Creation (Gen. 1–2)
2. The fall (Gen. 3)
3. Redemption (Gospels and Epistles as anticipated by the Old Testament)
4. Consummation (Gospels, Epistles, Revelation)

Consider Romans 8, a chapter where each of the four stages is discussed.

19. Jerry Bridges, *Growing Your Faith: How to Mature in Christ* (Colorado Springs: NavPress, 2004).

Implications:

1. It all belongs to God.
2. It is all tainted by rebellion against God.
3. Christ died and rose to restore the creation to God and to re-create God's image in us.
4. Jesus will return to complete the new creation, expelling all that has no place in it.

Case studies: Look at the texts cited and think of how what they say might change your thinking at the worldview level. What other passages come to your mind with regard to the subject?

Work: Colossians 3:17, 23

Human relations: 2 Corinthians 5:16

Economics: Haggai 1:5–6

Trends: Ecclesiastes 7:14

International crises: Psalm 37:1; Proverbs 21:1; Isaiah 40:15

Consider reading *Creation Regained* by Albert Wolters.[20]

13. Learning to Handle Hard Times

How should we respond to hard times?

(1) John 16:33; **(2)** Acts 14:22; **(3)** Romans 5:1–5; **(4)** James 1:2–4; **(5)** 2 Corinthians 7:4; **(6)** Romans 12:12; **(7)** 2 Corinthians 1:3–11; **(8)** Psalm 42; **(9)** 1 Peter 5:10–11; **(10)** 2 Corinthians 4:16–18; **(11)** Romans 8:18; **(12)** Hebrews 12:1–13

Consider reading *Walking with God through Pain and Suffering* by Timothy Keller.[21]

20. Albert M. Wolters, *Creation Regained: Biblical Basics for a Reformational Worldview*, 2nd ed. (Grand Rapids: Eerdmans, 2005).
21. Timothy Keller, *Walking with God through Pain and Suffering* (New York: Dutton, 2013).

8

BA (Biblical Agenda) in Christian Living

A Bible Study Resource for Discipling Others

The heart of this chapter is a study guide that may be used as is or adapted to your setting. The aim is to immerse growing disciples and prospective leaders in a book of the Bible so that they will see its relevance as delivered to us.[1] Some will choose to work through 2 Peter on their own before leading someone else to study it with them. Others will launch right in. The latter approach will foster the sense that both the leader and the one being discipled are on the same footing under the authority of the text of Scripture. If you are the preaching pastor of the church you serve, consider constructing a sermon series, as I did, that corresponds to the text's thought units selected here.

1. Those who favor topical preaching over consecutive exposition, or topic-based small-group Bible studies over working through a book of the Bible, sometimes do so because they have not heard good contextualized expositions from the pulpit or been part of a life-impacting inductive study of a biblical book.

Overview

2 Peter 1:1: What Is a Christian?

2 Peter 1:2: The Secret of Christian Living

2 Peter 1:3–9: The Antidote to Unfruitful Knowledge of God

2 Peter 1:10–11: The Christian's Horizons

2 Peter 1:12–15: Disciple Making

2 Peter 1:16–21: The Bible's Origin and Our Response

2 Peter 2:1–3: Counterattack

2 Peter 2:4–10a: Learning from Scripture: Character Studies

2 Peter 2:10b–16: Sin and Judgment

2 Peter 2:17–22: Backsliding

2 Peter 3:1–2: A Biblical Antidote to Spiritual Slippage

2 Peter 3:3–7: Dealing with Scoffers

2 Peter 3:8–13: Evangelism in the End Times

2 Peter 3:14–16: Making Every Effort

2 Peter 3:17–18: On Guard and Growing

A Word to Leaders

This outline for individual or very-small-group discipling is based on 2 Peter. Its purpose is to provide a framework by which a seasoned Christian can share specific ideas in Bible study methods and fellowship with a newer Christian into whose life he or she[2] is building scriptural truths. It has several advantages:

1. It is biblical. Instead of seeking to impose ideas on the text, it derives its content from the passage of Scripture.

2. Due to our convictions, we have envisioned current and potential *elders* as men throughout. We believe all other church leadership roles are open to women. And we don't really recommend men discipling women one-on-one. But this resource could lend itself to numerous uses, including contexts in which both men and women take part.

2. It is contextual. That is, biblical passages are not gathered from all parts of the scriptural text—though there is a place for that approach, as the parallel passages that are listed show—but are taken sequentially from a single letter of the New Testament.

3. It is flexible. The book may be studied, using the following guide, at a very elementary or a very sophisticated level, depending on the maturity of both the leader and the person who is being discipled.

4. It is transferrable. With a minimum of training and only this guide, or even without it, a person who has been discipled by working through 2 Peter can readily let it help him or her to disciple another person.

5. It is relatively comprehensive. That is, the subjects that are raised by the text of 2 Peter cover many of the important things that a young Christian needs to understand and embrace to function as a believer.

6. It is life oriented. By its very nature, Scripture speaks to our hearts so that our minds are converted and our lifestyles changed. The discipler merely presses home the stated or implied questions of the scriptural text in such a way that the person being discipled can respond to the call of God.

General Instructions

Use the questions, parallel passages, and other reference materials in this outline as a guide and a starting point. They have been provided to stimulate your own thinking, to keep you in the biblical text, and to force you to your knees in dependence on the Lord. Each session should be bathed in prayer. Interaction between the leader and the person being discipled should not be limited to the time you spend together in your weekly meeting.

This guide includes only some of the many possible questions relating to each lesson. Some of the questions may sound very elementary to Christians of long standing. Don't skip over them or speed through them; let the younger believer interact meaningfully with them.

Questions were prepared with reference to the Greek text, initially while using for English the NIV, and now revised with reference to the ESV (in hand) and the CSB (consulted). Therefore words used here may not appear in your translation of 2 Peter. I note deviations from the ESV when I think they are needed to enhance clarity or faithfulness.

The text of 2 Peter raises some interesting questions. If you are leading this study, I suggest that, before you begin, you read the introduction to 2 Peter in either the ESV Study Bible or the NIV Zondervan Study Bible. A little more detail is supplied in *An Introduction to the New Testament* by D. A. Carson and Douglas J. Moo.[3] Good commentaries tackle these problems at various levels. Newer and better ones are being published all the time. When you get ready to use this material, select one or two of them as recommended by someone you trust. The latest edition of D. A. Carson's *New Testament Commentary Survey* is a trustworthy source to consult.[4] David R. Helm's *1 & 2 Peter and Jude: Sharing Christ's Sufferings* in Crossway's Preaching the Word series provides excellent examples of how 2 Peter will preach to contemporary congregations.[5]

Consider attempting to memorize part or all of 2 Peter. That way, its contents will be readily available to you for meditation and obedience.

Depending on the individual you are discipling, you may want to ask the younger learner to read the passage before you meet and answer some of the key questions. Then your time together can focus on review and application.

Remember that your goal is to help your friend discover the truths of Scripture for himself or herself.

---

3. D. A. Carson and Douglas J. Moo, *An Introduction to the New Testament*, 2nd ed. (Grand Rapids: Zondervan, 2005), 654–68.

4. D. A. Carson, *New Testament Commentary Survey*, 7th ed. (Grand Rapids: Baker Academic, 2013).

5. David R. Helm, *1 & 2 Peter and Jude: Sharing Christ's Sufferings*, Preaching the Word (Wheaton: Crossway, 2008).

2 Peter 1:1: What Is a Christian?

How does Peter define "Christian"? By this definition, are you a Christian?

Who gets the credit when someone becomes a Christian?

How is Jesus described in this verse? How does this compare with how you think of Jesus?

What difference does Jesus's deity make?

What does this verse tell us about our faith? The NIV and NET translate a word for "equal value" in this verse with the word "precious." How precious is your faith to you? What difference do you think it would make to a first-century Gentile to be told that his faith was of equal value to that of a Jew?

Who is qualified to receive faith?

What have you received from Christ?

What should be the attitude of someone who has received faith?

Parallel passages: Romans 3:21–26; John 1:1–5; Romans 8:33–35; James 1:18

2 Peter 1:2: The Secret of Christian Living

What is grace?

What is peace?

How is peace related to grace?

How are they to be multiplied in the believer's life?

Is this statement a wish, blessing, prayer, greeting, admonition, benediction, or some combination of these?

How are knowing about God and knowing God related? What specific steps can one take to better know Christ as Lord?

Exercise: Do a word study on some forms of the word for "know" or "knowledge" in the New Testament. Begin with parallel passages closest to the passage being studied, and work out from there. Here are some of the occurrences in the New Testament: 2 Peter 1:3, 8; 2:20–21; Colossians 3:10; 1 Corinthians 13:12 (twice); Acts 3:10 ("recognized"); 19:34 ("realized"); Luke 1:4 ("certainty"); Mark 2:8 ("perceiving"); 6:33, 54 ("recognized").

How can one grow in knowledge of God?

Emphasis: It is vitally important to know Jesus as Lord.

Parallel passages: *Romans 5:1–5; Ephesians 2:8–10; Psalm 27:4; John 17:3; Philippians 3:7–16*

2 Peter 1:3–9: The Antidote to Unfruitful Knowledge of God

Who takes the initiative in making us holy?

Are we lacking anything necessary for godliness?

Put verse 4 into your own words.

How are you using the resources that God has already given you to accomplish that goal?

How do promises help us to grow?

Are you actively involved in memorizing Scripture?

What promises do you find most precious?

What promise is made to the person who works at godliness?

What is true of those who neglect godliness?

Emphasis: Becoming a Christian requires only that we receive a gift (grace); living the Christian life requires effort. God has given us everything we need for life and godliness. When we use what he has given, we become "fruitful" (effective, productive, reproducing) Christians.

Parallel passages: *1 Corinthians 12:13; 1 Corinthians 10:13; Jeremiah 29:11–14; Ephesians 2:8–10; Galatians 5:22–23; Romans 8:5–17*

2 Peter 1:10–11: The Christian's Horizons

To what point in the past does Peter encourage the reader to look back as his or her starting point?

What truth does the doctrine of election preserve?

What pitfalls await the Christian who selects another horizon—such as one's baptism, joining the church, or even one's decision for Christ—as his or her starting point?

According to verse 11, what future reality awaits those who are diligent to confirm their calling and election? From the context, how do we do that?

What does verse 11 promise will never happen to those who "practice these qualities"?

Emphasis: The Christian life is a race. Becoming a Christian is the starting line, not the finish line. Emphasize the importance of knowing

God's part and our part in the work of salvation. Assurance of salvation comes when we recall the past and future work of the Savior. Effort to grow in godliness is evidence of rebirth, not the basis of it.

Read *God's Words* (pp. 156–68) by J. I. Packer.[6]

Parallel passages: *Romans 8:28–30; Matthew 6:25–34; Philippians 2:12–13; 2 Timothy 4:1–18; 1 John 3:19–21; 5:10–12, 20; 2 Corinthians 13:5–6*

2 Peter 1:12–15: Disciple Making

What are the "these things" (CSB, NIV) of verses 12 and 15?

What is Peter's intention in writing "these things"?

Why do even those who are firmly established need reminders?

What are the characteristics of good discipling according to this passage?

Who could I be discipling?

Read *The Master Plan of Evangelism* by Robert Coleman.[7]

Parallel passages: *Matthew 28:18–20; Colossians 1:3–14; 2 Timothy 2:1–2*

2 Peter 1:16–21: The Bible's Origin and Our Response

What is the Bible according to Peter? What is it *not*?

Who is its subject?

6. J. I. Packer, *God's Words: Studies of Key Bible Themes* (Downers Grove, IL: InterVarsity, 1981).
7. Robert E. Coleman, *The Master Plan of Evangelism*, 2nd ed. (Grand Rapids: Revell, 2006).

How did it come to us?

What part did human beings play? Think of Peter's example as one writer of Scripture.

What part did the Holy Spirit play?

What should be our response to the Bible?

Parallel passages: *2 Timothy 3:15–17; Hebrews 4:12–13; 1 Peter 1:22–25; Matthew 5:17–18*

2 Peter 2:1–3: Counterattack

Where there is truth, there will also be _____.

How can we spot false teachers?

How do people deny Christ?

How do false teachings destroy people?

What effects will false teachings have?

What will overtake such false teachers?

How do we overcome false teaching?

Parallel passages: *Colossians, Galatians, 1 John, Jude, and other New Testament writings deal with specific false doctrines. As you are able, use them as illustrations of how biblical writers responded to falsehood.*

2 Peter 2:4–10a: Learning from Scripture: Character Studies

This passage is one long statement. What parts make up the protasis—the "if" part of the statement?

What part makes up the conclusion—the "then" part?

Which words describe some facet of salvation?

Which words describe judgment?

What sins are singled out for present punishment to be followed by eternal judgment?

What does this example teach us about how to use the Bible?

Emphasis: Notice how judgment and salvation are explained alongside each other.

Parallel passages: *The book of Jude is very similar to the content of the second chapter of 2 Peter. It is difficult to determine whether both Jude and Peter drew from a common source or one of them drew from the other. Check out a commentary, such as the one by Gene Green,[8] to see what some of the issues are. The main point is not to have the answers to difficult questions such as these but to help young Christians see that there are several possible good answers. Other parallel passages include Luke 17:26–29; Romans 1:18–23; Psalm 50.*

2 Peter 2:10b–16: Sin and Judgment

Emphasize one or two of the following descriptions of false teachers as you press home the nature of sin.

2:10	Arrogant, slanderers
2:12	Lacking understanding, blasphemous, brute beasts, destined for destruction
2:13	Distorted idea of pleasure
2:14	Insatiably seductive, experts in greed
2:15	Wanderers from the straight way, lovers of the ways of wickedness
2:16	Mad

8. Gene L. Green, *Jude and 2 Peter*, Baker Exegetical Commentary on the New Testament (Grand Rapids: Baker Academic, 2008).

What seem to be the root sins?

What is the basis and nature of God's judgment of sin (see verse 13a)?

Emphasis: Sin makes us animals.

Parallel passages: *James 1:26; 3:3–12; Numbers 22 (see especially verses 19, 32); Revelation 2:14; Psalm 50:20; Psalms 16–17*

2 Peter 2:17–22: Backsliding

How is backsliding described?

What practices are characteristic of it?

What is so terrible about backsliding?

What can we do to avoid backsliding?

How do we walk in the way of righteousness?

Emphasis: Backsliding is living a lie.

Parallel passages: *Hebrews 6:4–12; 10:2–39; Galatians 5:1; 1 Peter 1:3–9; Philippians 1:6*

2 Peter 3:1–2: A Biblical Antidote to Spiritual Slippage

What are we to recall to avoid the sins detailed in chapter 2?

How can we "stimulate . . . wholesome thinking" (NIV) or "stir up . . . sincere understanding" (CSB)?

Peter writes to stir up a "pure mind," as Young's Literal Translation puts it. It may be tempting to limit mental purity to things of a sexual nature. What else should we include in this concept?

What keeps us from single-mindedness?

Do a word study on "single-mindedness," which is sometimes translated "sincerity." See 1 Corinthians 5:8; 2 Corinthians 1:12; 2:17.

Parallel passages: 1 Timothy 1:5; Matthew 6:22–23;[9] Philippians 4:4–9; Psalm 119:11; Colossians 3:1–17; Matthew 4:19

2 Peter 3:3–7: Dealing with Scoffers

When are the "last days" (see Acts 2:16–17)?

What kind of things do scoffers say?

Why are they wrong?

What is the function of God's Word in the face of such scoffing (vv. 5, 7)?

How do we overcome lies?

How could Peter's approach be used to deal with those who give excuses for rejecting biblical claims?

Parallel passages: Psalm 1; Matthew 4:1–11; Romans 12:21; Jude 17–21; Acts 13:38–43

2 Peter 3:8–13: Evangelism in the End Times

What one thing can we count on as we survey the future?

9. Literally, "If your eye is single . . ."

Why is Christ's coming delayed?

What should we be doing in the meantime?

How can we speed or hasten the coming of the Lord?

Given the certainty of the destruction of the earth, what kinds of things should we value?

What difference should it make if I am looking forward to the coming of the Lord?

Emphasis: The urgency of evangelism

Parallel passages: Psalm 90:4;[10] John 21:18–23;[11] Acts 1:6–8; Amos 5; 1 John 3:1–3

2 Peter 3:14–16: Making Every Effort

What does this passage say to those who are complacently waiting around for Jesus to return?

Why is the delay of Christ's return a good thing?

How does Peter describe the apostle Paul's writings?

What factors contribute to the faulty interpretation?

What specific efforts should we make in light of the Lord's return?

Parallel passages: Psalm 15; 1 Corinthians 1:8; 1 Thessalonians 5:23; Proverbs 2:1–5

10. Notice the message of this psalm as a whole.
11. Note Peter's disinterest in signs.

2 Peter 3:17–18: On Guard and Growing

To what does Peter refer by the word "this" in verse 17?

Against what should we be on guard?

How can we best be on guard?

How can we grow?

Why do you suppose Peter uses the expression "fall from your secure position" (NIV)?

What will be the ultimate result from the lifestyle to which Peter exhorts his readers?

Parallel passages: *2 Corinthians 3:18; Matthew 5:14–16*

Acknowledgments

I (Greg) am especially grateful to the elders-in-training at Salem Evangelical Free Church of Fargo, North Dakota, for their patience and feedback as together we worked our way through earlier versions of this material. Their eager faithfulness remains an inspiration to me and a spur to put this material into a transferable and adaptable form. I learned a lot from them, and their insights and comments were incorporated into my notes for subsequent groups of elders-in-training and have found their way into this book. I acknowledge my indebtedness to them. Brian Vos and James Korsmo made many valuable suggestions and corrections. Ryan Fields graciously offered genuine expertise and helpful, specific, well-informed feedback on this material, and Will Hong helped once again with eagle-eyed editing. Graham and Rebecca Scharf and Dee Brestin offered wonderful writing places and, as always, my wife, Ruth, was there to share the exhilarating parts of this task—and the other parts too. The contribution of my many prayer partners is significant and much appreciated.

I (Arthur) am grateful to Greg Scharf for allowing me to be a part of this project. Greg has not only been a teacher to me at seminary and a constant encouragement, but he has also modeled what it means to combine a deep devotion to God's Word with an unwavering commitment to personal holiness. I'm honored to offer this book to God's people in partnership with him. My love for the gospel and the church would not be what it is without the personal investment of my pastors, Colin Smith and Scott Lothery. And my greatest thanks, unquestionably, goes to my wife, Weixiu. Without her rock-solid support, my involvement with this book would not have happened. Her prayers, love, and dedication to Jesus have bolstered my faith throughout our marriage. More than anyone, she reveals Christ to me.

Suggestions for Further Reading

Alcorn, Randy. *Managing God's Money: A Biblical Guide*. Wheaton: Tyndale, 2011.

———. *Money, Possessions, and Eternity*. Rev. ed. Wheaton: Tyndale, 2003. Anyone who teaches about money and possessions should read this book.

———. *The Purity Principle: God's Safeguards for Life's Dangerous Trails*. Colorado Springs: Multnomah, 2003.

———. *The Treasure Principle: Unlocking the Secret of Joyful Giving*. LifeChange Books. Rev. ed. Colorado Springs: Multnomah, 2005.

Allen, David. *Getting Things Done: The Art of Stress-Free Productivity*. Rev. ed. New York: Penguin, 2015.

Allender, Dan. *Leading with a Limp: Take Full Advantage of Your Most Powerful Weakness*. Colorado Springs: WaterBrook, 2008.

Allender, Dan B., and Tremper Longman III. *Breaking the Idols of Your Heart: How to Navigate the Temptations of Life*. Downers Grove, IL: InterVarsity, 2007.

———. *The Cry of the Soul: How Our Emotions Reveal Our Deepest Questions about God*. Colorado Springs: NavPress, 1999.

Allison, Gregg R. *Historical Theology: An Introduction to Christian Doctrine*. Grand Rapids: Zondervan, 2011.

———. *Sojourners and Strangers: The Doctrine of the Church*. Wheaton: Crossway, 2012.

Anderson, Neil. *The Bondage Breaker*. Eugene, OR: Harvest House, 2006.

Anyabwile, Thabiti M. *Finding Faithful Elders and Deacons*. Wheaton: Crossway, 2012.

———. *What Is a Healthy Church Member?* 9Marks. Wheaton: Crossway, 2008.

Arthurs, Jeffrey. *Devote Yourself to the Public Reading of Scripture: The Transforming Power of the Well-Spoken Word*. Grand Rapids: Kregel, 2012.

Axelrod, Dick, and Emily Axelrod. *Let's Stop Meeting Like This: Tools to Save Time and Get More Done*. San Francisco: Berrett-Koehler, 2014.

Bartholomew, Craig G., and Michael W. Goheen. *The Drama of Scripture: Finding Our Place in the Biblical Story*. 2nd ed. Grand Rapids: Baker Academic, 2014.

Baucham, Voddie, Jr. *Family Driven Faith: Doing What It Takes to Raise Sons and Daughters Who Walk with God*. Wheaton: Crossway, 2011.

———. *Family Shepherds: Calling and Equipping Men to Lead Their Homes*. Wheaton: Crossway, 2011.

Berghoef, Gerard, and Lester De Koster. *The Elder's Handbook: A Practical Guide for Church Leaders*. Grand Rapids: Christian's Library, 1979.

Blomberg, Craig L. *Can We Still Believe the Bible? An Evangelical Engagement with Contemporary Questions*. Grand Rapids: Brazos, 2014.

Boice, James Montgomery. *Foundations of the Christian Faith*. 2nd ed. Downers Grove, IL: InterVarsity, 1986.

Bonar, Andrew A. *The Visitor's Book of Texts: A Vital Tool for Pastoral Visitation*. Edinburgh, UK: Banner of Truth, 2010.

Bonhoeffer, Dietrich. *The Cost of Discipleship*. New York: Touchstone, 1965.

———. *Life Together*. New York: HarperCollins, 2009.

Borgman, Brian, and Rob Ventura. *Spiritual Warfare: A Biblical and Balanced Perspective*. Grand Rapids: Reformation Heritage Books, 2014.

Boston, Thomas. *Human Nature in Its Fourfold State*. Reprint, Edinburgh, UK: Banner of Truth Trust, 2015.

Brestin, Dee. *The Friendships of Women: The Beauty and Power of God's Plan for Us*. Colorado Springs: David C. Cook, 2008. Every man should read this book!

Bridges, Jerry. *The Blessing of Humility: Walk within Your Calling*. Colorado Springs: NavPress, 2016.

———. *The Discipline of Grace: God's Role and Our Role in the Pursuit of Holiness*. Colorado Springs: NavPress, 2006.

———. *The Gospel for Real Life: Turn to the Liberating Power of the Cross . . . Every Day*. Colorado Springs: NavPress, 2002.

———. *The Practice of Godliness*. Colorado Springs: NavPress, 2008.

———. *The Pursuit of Holiness*. Colorado Springs: NavPress, 2006.

———. *Respectable Sins: Confronting the Sins We Often Tolerate*. Colorado Springs: NavPress, 2007.

———. *Transforming Grace: Living Confidently in God's Unfailing Love*. Colorado Springs: NavPress, 2008.

Brooks, Thomas. *Precious Remedies against Satan's Devices*. Edinburgh, UK: Banner of Truth, 1968.

Brown, Harold O. J. *Heresies: Heresy and Orthodoxy in the History of the Church*. Peabody, MA: Hendrickson, 1998.

Bugbee, Bruce L. *What You Do Best in the Body of Christ: Discover Your Spiritual Gifts, Personal Style, and God-Given Passion*. Rev. ed. Grand Rapids: Zondervan, 2005.

Bugbee, Bruce L., and Don Cousins. *Network Participant's Guide: The Right People, in the Right Places, for the Right Reasons, at the Right Time*. Rev. ed. Grand Rapids: Zondervan, 2005.

Campbell, Ross. *How to Really Love Your Child*. 3rd ed. Colorado Springs: David C. Cook, 2015.

———. *How to Really Love Your Teen*. Rev. ed. Colorado Springs: David C. Cook, 2015.

Carson, D. A., ed. *The Enduring Authority of the Christian Scriptures*. Grand Rapids: Eerdmans, 2016.

———. *For the Love of God: A Daily Companion for Discovering the Riches of God's Word*. 2 vols. Wheaton: Crossway, 2006.

———. *New Testament Commentary Survey*. 7th ed. Grand Rapids: Baker Academic, 2013.

———. *Praying with Paul: A Call to Spiritual Reformation*. 2nd ed. of *A Call to Spiritual Reformation: Priorities from Paul and His Prayers*. Grand Rapids: Baker Academic, 2015.

Carson, D. A., and Douglas J. Moo. *An Introduction to the New Testament*. 2nd ed. Grand Rapids: Zondervan, 2005.

Carson, D. A., and John Woodbridge, eds. *Scripture and Truth*. 3rd ed. Grand Rapids: Baker, 1992.

Carter, Kori. *The Christian Athlete Training Journal: A 12 Week Workout, Nutrition, and Spiritual Logbook*. KC13 Corporation, 2016.

Challies, Tim. *Do More Better: A Practical Guide to Productivity*. Minneapolis: Cruciform, 2015.

Chambers, Oswald. *My Utmost for His Highest*. Classic ed. Uhrichsville, OH: Barbour, 2000.

Chan, Francis, and Preston Sprinkle. *Erasing Hell: What God Said about Eternity, and the Things We've Made Up*. Colorado Springs: David C. Cook, 2011.

Chapell, Bryan. *Christ-Centered Worship: Letting the Gospel Shape Our Practice*. Grand Rapids: Baker Academic, 2009.

———. *Holiness by Grace: Delighting in the Joy That Is Our Strength*. Wheaton: Crossway, 2001.

———. *Praying Backwards: Transform Your Prayer Life by Beginning in Jesus' Name*. Grand Rapids: Baker Books, 2005.

Charles, J. Daryl, ed. *Reading Genesis 1–2: An Evangelical Conversation*. Peabody, MA: Hendrickson, 2013.

Chester, Tim, and Steve Timmis. *Total Church: A Radical Reshaping around Gospel and Community*. Wheaton: Crossway, 2008.

"Chicago Statement on Biblical Inerrancy." 1978. Available online at http://www.bible-researcher.com/chicago1.html.

Cole, Graham. *He Who Gives Life: The Doctrine of the Holy Spirit*. Foundations of Evangelical Theology. Wheaton: Crossway, 2007.

Coleman, Robert E. *The Master Plan of Evangelism*. 2nd ed. Grand Rapids: Revell, 2006.

Collins, Gary R. *Christian Counseling: A Comprehensive Guide*. 3rd ed. Nashville: Thomas Nelson, 2007.

Colson, Charles, and Nancy Pearcey. *How Now Shall We Live?* Wheaton: Tyndale, 1999.

Cosper, Mike. *Rhythms of Grace: How the Church's Worship Tells the Story of the Gospel*. Wheaton: Crossway, 2013.

Cousins, Don. *Experiencing LeaderShift: Letting Go of Leadership Heresies*. 2nd ed. Colorado Springs: David C. Cook, 2008.

Crouch, Andy. *Culture Making: Recovering Our Creative Calling*. Downers Grove, IL: InterVarsity, 2013.

———. *The Tech-Wise Family: Everyday Steps for Putting Technology in Its Proper Place.* Grand Rapids: Baker Books, 2017.

Dayton, Howard L. *Your Money Counts: The Biblical Guide to Earning, Spending, Saving, Investing, Giving, and Getting Out of Debt.* Wheaton: Tyndale, 2011.

DeLashmutt, Gary. *Loving God's Way: A Fresh Look at the One Another Passages.* Columbus, OH: Xenos, 2007.

Demarest, Bruce. *The Cross and Salvation: The Doctrine of Salvation.* Foundations of Evangelical Theology. Wheaton: Crossway, 1997.

———. *Who Is Jesus? Further Reflections on Jesus Christ: The God-Man.* 1984. Reprint, Eugene, OR: Wipf & Stock, 2008.

Dever, Mark. *The Gospel and Personal Evangelism.* Wheaton: Crossway, 2007.

Dever, Mark, and Paul Alexander. *The Deliberate Church: Building Your Ministry on the Gospel.* Wheaton: Crossway, 2005.

DeYoung, Kevin. *Crazy Busy: A (Mercifully) Short Book about a (Really) Big Problem.* Wheaton: Crossway, 2013.

———. *The Hole in Our Holiness: Filling the Gap between Gospel Passion and the Pursuit of Godliness.* Wheaton: Crossway, 2012.

———. *The Holy Spirit.* Gospel Coalition Booklets. Wheaton: Crossway, 2011.

———. *Just Do Something: A Liberating Approach to Finding God's Will.* Chicago: Moody, 2014.

———. *Taking God at His Word: Why the Bible Is Knowable, Necessary, and Enough, and What That Means for You and Me.* Wheaton: Crossway, 2016.

———. *What Does the Bible Really Teach about Homosexuality?* Wheaton: Crossway, 2015.

DeYoung, Kevin, and Ted Kluck. *Why We Love the Church: In Praise of Institutions and Organized Religion.* Chicago: Moody, 2009.

Dickson, David. *The Elder and His Work.* Edited by George Kennedy McFarland and Philip Graham Ryken. Phillipsburg, NJ: P&R, 2004.

Dickson, John. *Humilitas: A Lost Key to Life, Love, and Leadership.* Grand Rapids: Zondervan, 2011.

Donahue, Bill. *Leading Life-Changing Small Groups.* Groups That Grow. 3rd ed. Grand Rapids: Zondervan, 2012.

Doriani, Dan. *The New Man: Becoming a Man after God's Heart.* Phillipsburg, NJ: P&R, 2015.

———. *Putting the Truth to Work: The Theory and Practice of Biblical Application.* Phillipsburg, NJ: P&R, 2001.

Duguid, Barbara R., and Wayne Duguid Houk. *Prone to Wander: Prayers of Confession and Celebration.* Phillipsburg, NJ: P&R, 2014.

Edwards, David L., and John R. W. Stott. *Evangelical Essentials: A Liberal-Evangelical Dialogue.* 1988. Reprint, Downers Grove, IL: InterVarsity, 1989.

Edwards, Jonathan. "The Resolutions of Jonathan Edwards." http://www.desiringgod.org/articles/the-resolutions-of-jonathan-edwards.

Elmer, Duane. *Cross-Cultural Servanthood: Serving the World in Christlike Humility.* Downers Grove, IL: InterVarsity, 2006.

Emerson, Michael, and Christian Smith. *Divided by Faith: Evangelical Religion and the Problem of Race in America*. New York: Oxford University Press, 2001.

Erickson, Millard J. *Christian Theology*. 3rd ed. Grand Rapids: Baker Academic, 2013.

Farley, William P. *Gospel-Powered Parenting: How the Gospel Shapes and Transforms Parenting*. Phillipsburg, NJ: P&R, 2009.

Fee, Gordon D., and Douglas Stuart. *How to Read the Bible for All Its Worth*. 4th ed. Grand Rapids: Zondervan, 2014.

Feinberg, John S., and Paul D. Feinberg. *Ethics for a Brave New World*. 2nd ed. Wheaton: Crossway, 2010.

Ford, Leighton. *Transforming Leadership: Jesus' Way of Creating Vision, Shaping Values & Empowering Change*. Downers Grove, IL: InterVarsity, 1993.

Furman, Gloria C. *Glimpses of Grace: Treasuring the Gospel in Your Home*. Wheaton: Crossway, 2013.

Getz, Gene. *Building Up One Another*. One Another Series. Colorado Springs: David C. Cook, 2002.

Gilbert, Greg. *What Is the Gospel?* Wheaton: Crossway, 2010.

Greear, J. D. *Jesus, Continued . . . : Why the Spirit inside You Is Better than Jesus beside You*. Grand Rapids: Zondervan, 2014.

Grudem, Wayne. *Bible Doctrine: Essential Teachings of the Christian Faith*. Edited by Jeff Purswell. Grand Rapids: Zondervan, 1999. The so-called Baby Grudem is a succinct version of the 1994 volume.

———. *Systematic Theology: An Introduction to Biblical Doctrine*. Grand Rapids: Zondervan, 1994. This remains a highly influential source.

Guthrie, Nancy. *What Grieving People Wish You Knew about What Really Helps (and What Really Hurts)*. Wheaton: Crossway, 2016.

Harris, Joshua. *Sex Is Not the Problem (Lust Is): Sexual Purity in a Lust-Saturated World*. Colorado Springs: Multnomah, 2005.

Harris, Murray J. *Jesus as God: The New Testament Use of* Theos *in Reference to Jesus*. 1992. Reprint, Eugene, OR: Wipf & Stock, 2008.

Hill, Megan. *Praying Together: The Priority and Privilege of Prayer*. Wheaton: Crossway, 2016.

Hindson, Edward, ed. *An Introduction to Puritan Theology: A Reader*. Grand Rapids: Guardian, 1976.

Hoffmeier, James K. *The Immigration Crisis: Immigrants, Aliens, and the Bible*. Wheaton: Crossway, 2009.

Holcomb, Justin S. *Know the Creeds and Councils*. Know Series. Grand Rapids: Zondervan, 2014.

———. *Know the Heretics*. Know Series. Grand Rapids: Zondervan, 2014.

Holmes, Jonathan. *The Company We Keep: In Search of Biblical Friendship*. Minneapolis: Cruciform, 2014.

Hoover, Christine. *Messy Beautiful Friendship: Finding and Nurturing Deep and Lasting Relationships*. Grand Rapids: Baker Books, 2017.

Horton, Michael. *The Christian Faith: A Systematic Theology for Pilgrims on the Way*. Grand Rapids: Zondervan, 2011.

Hughes, R. Kent. *Disciplines of a Godly Man*. 10th anniv. ed. Wheaton: Crossway, 2001.

Inrig, Gary. *Quality Friendship.* Chicago: Moody, 1988.

Jamieson, Bobby. *Sound Doctrine: How a Church Grows in the Love and Holiness of God.* 9Marks. Wheaton: Crossway, 2013.

———. *Understanding the Lord's Supper.* Nashville: B&H, 2016.

Jensen, Phillip D., and Tony Payne. *Guidance and the Voice of God.* Rev. ed. Kingsford, NSW: Matthias Media, 2012.

Jones, Mark. *Faith. Hope. Love. The Christ-Centered Way to Grow in Grace.* Wheaton: Crossway, 2017.

———. *God Is: A Devotional Guide to the Attributes of God.* Wheaton: Crossway, 2017.

Jones, Robert D. *Forgiveness: I Just Can't Forgive Myself.* Resources for Changing Lives. Phillipsburg, NJ: P&R, 2000.

Jones, Thomas, and Steve Brown. *One Another: Transformational Relationships in the Body of Christ.* Spring Hill, TN: DPI Books, 2008.

Kaiser, Walter C., Jr., and Moisés Silva. *Introduction to Biblical Hermeneutics: The Search for Meaning.* Rev. ed. Grand Rapids: Zondervan, 2007.

Kang, Joshua Choonmin. *Scripture by Heart: Devotional Practices for Memorizing God's Word.* Downers Grove, IL: InterVarsity, 2010.

Kauflin, Bob. *Worship Matters: Leading Others to Encounter the Greatness of God.* Wheaton: Crossway, 2008.

Keller, Timothy. *Counterfeit Gods: The Empty Promises of Money, Sex, and Power, and the Only Hope That Matters.* New York: Penguin, 2011.

———. *Encountering Jesus: Unexpected Answers to Life's Biggest Questions.* New York: Dutton, 2013.

———. *Every Good Endeavor: Connecting Your Work to God's Work.* New York: Penguin, 2012.

———. *The Meaning of Marriage: Facing the Complexities of Commitment with the Wisdom of God.* New York: Dutton, 2011.

———. *Prayer: Experiencing Awe and Intimacy with God.* New York: Dutton, 2014.

Kilner, John F., ed. *Why the Church Needs Bioethics: A Guide to Wise Engagement with Life's Challenges.* Grand Rapids: Zondervan, 2011.

Klein, William W., Craig L. Blomberg, and Robert L. Hubbard Jr. *Introduction to Biblical Interpretation.* 3rd ed. Grand Rapids: Zondervan, 2017.

Koesler, John, ed. *Foundational Faith: Unchangeable Truth for an Ever-Changing World.* Chicago: Moody, 2003.

Köstenberger, Andreas J., and David W. Jones. *God, Marriage, and Family: Rebuilding the Biblical Foundation.* 2nd ed. Wheaton: Crossway, 2010.

Kruis, John G. *Quick Scripture Reference for Counseling.* 3rd ed. Grand Rapids: Baker Books, 2001.

Lambert, Heath. *Finally Free: Fighting for Purity with the Power of Grace.* Grand Rapids: Zondervan, 2013.

Lane, Timothy S., and Paul David Tripp. *How People Change.* Greensboro, NC: New Growth, 2006.

———. *Relationships: A Mess Worth Making.* Greensboro, NC: New Growth, 2008.

Leeman, Jonathan. *Church Discipline: How the Church Protects the Name of Jesus.* 9Marks. Wheaton: Crossway, 2012.

———. *Church Membership: How the World Knows Who Represents Jesus.* 9Marks. Wheaton: Crossway, 2012.

———. *Word-Centered Church: How Scripture Brings Life and Growth to God's People.* Chicago: Moody, 2017.

Lencioni, Patrick. *Death by Meeting: A Leadership Fable . . . about Solving the Most Painful Problem in Business.* San Francisco: Jossey-Bass, 2004.

Lewis, Gordon R. *Decide for Yourself: A Theological Workbook.* 1970. Reprint, Eugene, OR: Wipf & Stock, 2012. The inductive approach this volume models inspired the pedagogical approach underlying the present volume.

Lloyd-Jones, D. Martyn. *Authority.* Edinburgh, UK: Banner of Truth, 1984.

———. *Spiritual Depression: Its Causes and Its Cure.* Grand Rapids: Eerdmans, 1965.

Luther, Martin. *Christians Can Be Soldiers.* Edited by Paul Strawn. Translated by Holger Sonntag. Minneapolis: Lutheran Press, 2010.

MacArthur, John. *Found: God's Will.* 3rd ed. Elgin, IL: David C. Cook, 2012.

———. *The Power of Integrity: Building a Life without Compromise.* Wheaton: Crossway, 1997.

MacDonald, Gordon. *The Effective Father.* 9th ed. Wheaton: Tyndale, 1977.

Marshall, Colin, and Tony Payne. *The Trellis and the Vine: The Ministry Mind-Shift That Changes Everything.* Kingsford, NSW: Matthias Media, 2009.

McComiskey, Thomas Edward. *Reading Scripture in Public: A Guide for Preachers and Lay Readers.* Grand Rapids: Baker, 1991.

McLean, Max. *Unleashing the Word: Rediscovering the Public Reading of Scripture.* Grand Rapids: Zondervan, 2009.

Meade, Starr. *Give Them Truth: Teaching Eternal Truths to Young Minds.* Phillipsburg, NJ: P&R, 2015.

Merkle, Benjamin L. *40 Questions about Elders and Deacons.* Grand Rapids: Kregel, 2008.

———. *Why Elders? A Biblical and Practical Guide for Church Members.* Grand Rapids: Kregel Academic & Professional, 2009.

Metzger, Will. *Tell the Truth: The Whole Gospel to the Whole Person by Whole People.* Downers Grove, IL: InterVarsity, 1984.

Miller, Paul E. *A Praying Life: Connecting with God in a Distracting World.* Colorado Springs: NavPress, 2009.

Miller, Samuel. *Thoughts on Public Prayer.* Charleston, SC: BiblioLife, 2009.

Milne, Bruce. *Know the Truth: A Handbook of Christian Belief.* 3rd ed. Downers Grove, IL: InterVarsity, 2009.

Minear, Paul Sevier. *Images of the Church in the New Testament.* New Testament Library. Louisville: Westminster John Knox, 2004.

Minirth, Frank, Paul D. Meier, and Don Hawkins. *How to Beat Burnout.* Chicago: Moody, 1986.

Moeller, Robert. *Love in Action: Dealing with Conflict in Your Church.* Sisters, OR: Multnomah, 1994.

Mohler, R. Albert, Jr. *The Conviction to Lead: 25 Principles for Leadership That Matters*. Minneapolis: Bethany House, 2012.

Morris, Leon. *The Apostolic Preaching of the Cross*. 3rd ed. Grand Rapids: Eerdmans, 1955.

Murray, Andrew. *Humility: The Beauty of Holiness*. Updated ed. Abbotsford, WI: Aneko Press, 2016.

The Navigators. *Topical Memory System*. Carol Stream, IL: NavPress, 2006.

Nelson, Tom. *Work Matters: Connecting Sunday Worship to Monday Work*. Wheaton: Crossway, 2011.

Newbell, Trillia J. *United: Captured by God's Vision of Diversity*. Chicago: Moody, 2014.

Newton, John. "On Controversy" [sometimes also titled "A Guide to Godly Disputation"]. In *Letters of John Newton*, 377. 1869. Reprint, Edinburgh, UK: Banner of Truth, 2007.

Newton, Phil A., and Matt Schmucker. *Elders in the Life of the Church: Rediscovering the Biblical Model for Church Leadership*. Rev. ed. Grand Rapids: Kregel Ministry, 2014.

Oden, Thomas C. *John Wesley's Teachings*. Vol. 3, *Pastoral Theology*. Grand Rapids: Zondervan, 2012.

Olyott, Stuart. *Reading the Bible and Praying in Public*. Edinburgh, UK: Banner of Truth, 2008.

Packer, J. I. *Concise Theology: A Guide to Historic Christian Beliefs*. Wheaton: Tyndale, 2001.

———. *Evangelism and the Sovereignty of God*. 1961. Americanized ed., Downers Grove, IL: InterVarsity, 2008.

———. *Faithfulness and Holiness: The Witness of J. C. Ryle; Including the Full Text of the First Edition of Ryle's Classic Book, "Holiness."* Wheaton: Crossway, 2002.

———. *God's Words: Studies of Key Bible Themes*. Downers Grove, IL: InterVarsity, 1981.

———. *Keeping the Ten Commandments*. Wheaton: Crossway, 2008.

———. *Keep in Step with the Spirit: Finding Fullness in Our Walk with God*. Rev. ed. Grand Rapids: Baker Books, 2005.

———. *Praying the Lord's Prayer*. Wheaton: Crossway, 2007.

Palmer, Nate. *Servanthood as Worship: The Privilege of Life in a Local Church*. Minneapolis: Cruciform, 2010.

Patrick, Darrin, and Amie Patrick. *The Dude's Guide to Marriage: Ten Skills Every Husband Must Develop to Love His Wife Well*. Nashville: Thomas Nelson, 2015.

Perman, Matt. *What's Best Next: How the Gospel Transforms the Way You Get Things Done*. 2nd ed. Grand Rapids: Zondervan, 2016.

Peterson, Jim, et al. *The Scriptural Roots of Ministry*. Version 2.1. Colorado Springs: The Navigators, 1992.

Peterson, Robert A. *Hell on Trial: The Case for Eternal Punishment*. Phillipsburg, NJ: P&R, 1995.

Piper, John. *Brothers, We Are Not Professionals: A Plea to Pastors for Radical Ministry*. Rev. ed. Nashville: B&H, 2013.

———. *A Hunger for God: Desiring God through Fasting and Prayer*. Wheaton: Crossway, 2013.

————. *Jesus: The Only Way to God: Must You Hear the Gospel to Be Saved?* Grand Rapids: Baker Books, 2010.

————. *The Marks of a Spiritual Leader.* Minneapolis: Desiring God, 2014.

————. *When the Darkness Will Not Lift: Doing What We Can While We Wait for God—and Joy.* Wheaton: Crossway, 2006.

Piper, John, and Justin Taylor, eds. *The Power of Words and the Wonder of God.* Wheaton: Crossway, 2009.

Pippert, Rebecca Manley. *Out of the Saltshaker and into the World: Evangelism as a Way of Life.* Downers Grove, IL: InterVarsity, 1979.

Platt, David. *Follow Me: A Call to Die. A Call to Live.* Wheaton: Tyndale, 2013.

Powlison, David. "Does the Shoe Fit?" *Journal of Biblical Counseling* 20, no. 3 (Spring 2002): 2–14.

————. *Good and Angry: Redeeming Anger, Irritation, Complaining and Bitterness.* Greensboro, NC: New Growth, 2016.

————. *Seeing with New Eyes: Counseling and the Human Condition through the Lens of Scripture.* Phillipsburg, NJ: P&R, 2003.

————. *Speaking Truth in Love: Counsel in Community.* Greensboro, NC: New Growth, 2005.

————. *Stress: Peace amid Pressure.* Resources for Changing Lives. Phillipsburg, NJ: P&R, 2004.

————. *Worry: Pursuing a Better Path to Peace.* Resources for Changing Lives. Phillipsburg, NJ: P&R, 2004.

Pratt, Richard L. *Praying with Your Eyes Open: Looking at God, Ourselves, and Our Prayers.* 2nd ed. Phillipsburg, NJ: P&R, 1987.

Priolo, Lou. *Deception: Letting Go of Lying.* Resources for Biblical Living. Phillipsburg, NJ: P&R, 2008.

Rainey, Dennis. *Stepping Up: A Call to Courageous Manhood.* Little Rock, AR: FamilyLife, 2011.

Raveling, Barbara. *The Renewing of the Mind Project: Going to God for Help with Your Habits, Goals and Emotions.* Hamilton, MT: Truthway, 2016.

Reinke, Tony. *12 Ways Your Phone Is Changing You.* Wheaton: Crossway, 2017.

Rinne, Jeramie. *Church Elders: How to Shepherd God's People Like Jesus.* 9Marks. Wheaton: Crossway, 2014. This volume is an excellent short summary of what lay elders are called to do.

Roberts, Vaughn. *God's Big Picture: Tracing the Storyline of the Bible.* Downers Grove, IL: InterVarsity, 2002.

————. *Talking Points: Transgender.* Epsom, UK: The Good Book Company, 2016.

————. *True Friendship.* Leyland, UK: 10Publishing, 2013.

Ryken, Leland, James C. Wilhoit, and Tremper Longman III, eds. *Dictionary of Biblical Imagery.* Downers Grove, IL: InterVarsity, 1998. This exceptional volume has a detailed Scripture index to help you see biblical images in any text you are studying or preaching.

Ryken, Philip Graham. *City on a Hill: Reclaiming the Biblical Pattern for the Church in the 21st Century.* New ed. Chicago: Moody, 2003. This volume lives up to its title.

Sande, Ken. *The Peacemaker: A Biblical Guide to Resolving Personal Conflict.* 3rd ed. Grand Rapids: Baker Books, 2004.

Sande, Ken, and Kevin Johnson. *Resolving Everyday Conflict*. Grand Rapids: Baker Books, 2015.

Sanders, Fred. *The Deep Things of God: How the Trinity Changes Everything*. Wheaton: Crossway, 2010.

Sanders, J. Oswald. *Spiritual Leadership: Principles of Excellence for Every Believer*. Rev. ed. Chicago: Moody, 2007.

Scharf, Greg. *Let the Earth Hear His Voice: Strategies for Overcoming Bottlenecks in Preaching God's Word*. Phillipsburg, NJ: P&R, 2015.

Schreiner, Thomas R. *New Testament Theology: Magnifying God in Christ*. Grand Rapids: Baker Academic, 2008.

Schreiner, Thomas R., and Ardel B. Caneday. *The Race Set before Us: A Biblical Theology of Perseverance & Assurance*. Downers Grove, IL: InterVarsity, 2001.

Schreiner, Thomas R., and Matthew R. Crawford. *The Lord's Supper: Remembering and Proclaiming Christ until He Comes*. New American Commentary Studies in Bible & Theology 10. Nashville: B&H, 2010.

Shaw, Robert. *The Reformed Faith: An Exposition of the Westminster Confession of Faith*. Rev. ed. Ross-shire, UK: Christian Focus, 2008.

Sherman, Amy L. *Kingdom Calling: Vocational Stewardship for the Common Good*. Downers Grove, IL: InterVarsity, 2012.

Short, David, and David Searle. *Pastoral Visitation: A Pocket Manual*. Ross-shire, UK: Christian Focus, 2015.

Smallman, Stephen. *The Walk: Steps for New and Renewed Followers of Jesus*. Phillipsburg, NJ: P&R, 2009.

Smith, Colin S. *The 10 Greatest Struggles of Your Life: Finding Freedom in God's Commands*. Chicago: Moody, 2006.

Sproul, R. C. *Abortion: A Rational Look at an Emotional Issue*. 2nd ed. Lake Mary, FL: Reformation Trust, 2010.

———. *Can I Know God's Will?* Lake Mary, FL: Reformation Trust, 2009.

———. *Everyone's a Theologian: An Introduction to Systematic Theology*. Sanford, FL: Reformation Trust, 2014.

———. *The Prayer of the Lord*. Lake Mary, FL: Reformation Trust, 2009.

———. *What Can I Do with My Guilt?* Crucial Questions 9. Sanford, FL: Reformation Trust, 2011.

Stiles, Mack J. *Speaking of Jesus: How to Tell Your Friends the Best News They Will Ever Hear*. Downers Grove, IL: InterVarsity, 1995.

Storms, Sam. *The Beginner's Guide to Spiritual Gifts*. Minneapolis: Bethany House, 2013.

Stott, John R. W. *Baptism and Fullness: The Work of the Holy Spirit Today*. 3rd ed. Downers Grove, IL: InterVarsity, 2006.

———. *Confess Your Sins: The Way of Reconciliation*. 1964. Reprint, Grand Rapids: Eerdmans, 2017.

———. *The Cross of Christ*. 20th anniv. ed. Downers Grove, IL: InterVarsity, 2006.

———. *The Grace of Giving: 10 Principles of Christian Giving*. The Didasko Files. 2004. Reprint, Peabody, MA: Hendrickson, 2012.

———. *Same Sex Relationships*. Epsom, UK: The Good Book Company, 2017.

Strand, Gregory, and William Kynes. *Evangelical Convictions: A Theological Exposition of the Statement of Faith of the Evangelical Free Church of America*. Minneapolis: Free Church Publications, 2011.

Strauch, Alexander. *Biblical Eldership: An Urgent Call to Restore Biblical Church Leadership*. 2nd ed. Littleton, CO: Lewis and Roth, 1995. This is the classic work on eldership and comes with a study guide. Strauch's research and conclusions are foundational.

———. *If You Bite and Devour One Another: Biblical Principles for Handling Conflict*. Littleton, CO: Lewis and Roth, 2011.

———. *Meetings That Work: A Guide to Effective Elders' Meetings*. Littleton, CO: Lewis and Roth, 2001.

———. *The New Testament Deacon: The Church's Minister of Mercy*. Littleton, CO: Lewis and Roth, 1992.

Tamminga, Louis M. *The Elder's Handbook*. Grand Rapids: Faith Alive, 2009, 2016.

Thompson, Rick. *E3: Effective, Empowering Elders*. St. Charles, IL: ChurchSmart, 2006.

Thune, Robert H. *Gospel Eldership: Equipping a New Generation of Servant Leaders*. Greensboro, NC: New Growth, 2016. This excellent workbook is for individuals being trained in the context of a small group. It focuses on character. I (Greg) have worked through this volume with my formation group at Trinity and profited by it personally.

Tidball, Derek J. *Builders and Fools: Leadership the Bible Way*. Leicester, UK: InterVarsity, 1999.

Tozer, A. W. *The Knowledge of the Holy: The Attributes of God*. New York: HarperCollins, 1961.

Trent, John, and Gary Smalley. *The Blessing: Giving the Gift of Unconditional Love and Acceptance*. Rev. ed. Nashville: Thomas Nelson, 2011.

Tripp, Paul David. *Dangerous Calling: Confronting the Unique Challenges of Pastoral Ministry*. Wheaton: Crossway, 2012.

———. *Instruments in the Redeemer's Hands: People in Need of Change Helping People in Need of Change*. Phillipsburg, NJ: P&R, 2002.

———. *New Morning Mercies: A Daily Gospel Devotional*. Wheaton: Crossway, 2014.

———. *Parenting: 14 Gospel Principles That Can Radically Change Your Family*. Wheaton: Crossway, 2016.

———. *Sex and Money: Pleasures That Leave You Empty and Grace That Satisfies*. Wheaton: Crossway, 2013.

———. *War of Words: Getting to the Heart of Your Communication Struggles*. Phillipsburg, NJ: P&R, 2000.

———. *What Did You Expect? Redeeming the Realities of Marriage*. Wheaton: Crossway, 2010.

Van Dam, Cornelis. *The Deacon: The Biblical Roots and the Ministry of Mercy Today*. Grand Rapids: Reformation Heritage Books, 2016.

Van Yperen, Jim. *Making Peace: A Guide to Overcoming Church Conflict*. 2nd ed. Chicago: Moody, 2002.

———. *Strategic Leadership Formation: Growing Character and Competence in Spiritual Leaders*. St. Charles, IL: ChurchSmart Resources, n.d.

Wagner, Maurice. *The Sensation of Being Somebody*. Grand Rapids: Zondervan, 1975.

Wald, Oletta. *The New Joy of Discovery in Bible Study*. Rev. ed. Minneapolis: Augsburg Fortress, 2002.

Waltke, Bruce. *Finding the Will of God: A Pagan Notion?* 2nd ed. Grand Rapids: Eerdmans, 2016.

Ward, Timothy. *Words of Life: Scripture as the Living and Active Word of God*. Downers Grove, IL: InterVarsity, 2009.

Wax, Trevin. *Gospel-Centered Teaching: Showing Christ in All the Scripture*. Nashville: B&H, 2013.

Welch, Edward T. *Addictions: A Banquet in the Grave: Finding Hope in the Power of the Gospel*. Resources for Changing Lives. Phillipsburg, NJ: P&R, 2001.

———. *Depression: The Way Up When You Are Down*. Resources for Changing Lives. Phillipsburg, NJ: P&R, 2000.

———. *"Just One More": When Desires Don't Take No for an Answer*. Resources for Changing Lives. Phillipsburg, NJ: P&R, 2002.

———. *Shame Interrupted: How God Lifts the Pain of Worthlessness and Rejection*. Greensboro, NC: New Growth, 2012.

———. *Side by Side: Walking with Others in Wisdom and Love*. Wheaton: Crossway, 2015.

———. *When I Am Afraid: A Step-by-Step Guide Away from Fear and Anxiety*. Greensboro, NC: New Growth, 2008.

———. *When People Are Big and God Is Small: Overcoming Peer Pressure, Codependency, and the Fear of Man*. Phillipsburg, NJ: P&R, 1997.

Wellum, Stephen J. *God the Son Incarnate: The Doctrine of Christ*. Foundations of Evangelical Theology. Wheaton: Crossway, 2016.

Whitney, Donald S. *Family Worship*. Wheaton: Crossway, 2016.

———. *Praying the Bible*. Wheaton: Crossway, 2015.

———. *Spiritual Disciplines for the Christian Life*. Rev. ed. Colorado Springs: NavPress, 2014.

Wiersbe, Warren W. *On Earth as It Is in Heaven: How the Lord's Prayer Teaches Us to Pray More Effectively*. Grand Rapids: Baker Books, 2010.

Witmer, Timothy Z. *The Shepherd Leader at Home: Knowing, Leading, Protecting, and Providing for Your Family*. Wheaton: Crossway, 2012.

Wolters, Albert M. *Creation Regained: Biblical Basics for a Reformational Worldview*. 2nd ed. Grand Rapids: Eerdmans, 2005.

Wolterstorff, Nicholas. *Lament for a Son*. Grand Rapids: Eerdmans, 1987.

Woodrow, Jonny, and Tim Chester. *The Ascension: Humanity in the Presence of God*. Ross-shire, UK: Christian Focus, 2013.

Wright, Christopher J. H. *Knowing the Holy Spirit through the Old Testament*. Downers Grove, IL: InterVarsity, 2006.

———. *Life through God's Word: Psalm 119*. Milton Keynes, UK: Authentic Lifestyle, 2006.

———. *The Mission of God's People: A Biblical Theology of the Church's Mission*. Grand Rapids: Zondervan, 2010.

Yancey, Philip. *Prayer: Does It Make Any Difference?* Grand Rapids: Zondervan, 2005.